Filigree's Rule

by

M Crane Hana

While every precaution has been taken in the preparation of this book, the publisher assumes no responsibility for errors or omissions, or for damages resulting from the use of the information contained herein.

FILIGREE'S RULE

First edition. April 26, 2021.

ISBN: 979-8201149383

Written by M. Crane Hana.

Table of Contents

Author's Note

If you think the publishing industry seems like a hostile, bewildering wasteland, you're not alone.

It doesn't have to be that mystifying, infuriating, or dangerous.

This book is a compilation of red flags, subtle clues, and other warning signs about publishing, begun in 2012 as a series of blog posts.

In reality it began back in the mid 1990s, when my writing 'reach' so thoroughly exceeded my grasp that I disappointed an agent who wanted to sell my fictional work. I just wasn't competent enough to write it, yet. It took six or so years for both of us to realize that and amicably part ways. By then I had shelved my original fiction in favor of a career in art manufacturing and technical writing. (I got back into fiction in 2009, and my first novel was published in 2012.)

During the decade-long hiatus I kept my attention on science-fiction, fantasy, and romance publishing, and how they were changing. I've been reading this stuff since 1976, so I've witnessed some amazing shifts in the publishing world. Many of the same bad-actor trends and tropes hold true in other literary genres, and show up in other cultural aspects of modern life.

I hope that by reading about the mistakes I've made and seen, new writers will develop the skepticism, research skills, and perseverance to find a safer, saner, and hopefully more fulfilling publishing path for themselves.

I will mention people and publishers in this book as case studies, the facts of which are readily available online. I mean no malice or disrespect in these mentions. I am simply using these events as examples of larger phenomena in publishing.

INTRODUCTION: Filigree's Rule

Filigree's Rule is simply this: "Some Authors Deserve Some Publishers...and I'm not going to stand in their way anymore."

Hi, I'm Filigree.

I've been Filigree online since the early 1990s.

I'm a fantasy writer, artist, jeweler, costumer, and welder. I've written original fiction, fanfiction, and technical non-fiction since 1987. If you're curious about my fanfiction, I'm 'Filigree' on Archive of Our Own., too. No, you won't have heard of my non-fiction writing, since that is all work-for-hire for specific companies.

This book is mostly about fiction and poetry publishing.

It isn't going to be a 'normal' happy, supportive cheerleading-type book about writing.

It won't teach you how to make a living at writing genre fiction, how to get your work represented by a capable literary agent, or how to become a best-selling self-published or commercially-published author.

This book is about mistakes, wishful thinking, warning signs, scams, con artists and their favorite victims, publishers too big to fail, the icebergs in their path, unprofessional publishers, terrible agents, clueless agents, and the rise of real and powerful publishing alternatives.

At best, this book will be about how not to lose hard-earned money in this business.

I have no sides in this game now: I'm self-publishing a large sprawling space-fantasy series that cannot be queried to any agent or large commercial publisher (due to two of my mistakes). If I write something that seems better suited to commercial publishing, damn right I'm going to query that thing to an agent!

Self-publishing and commercial publishing are just two choices in a large portfolio available to authors in the 2020s. With the exception of vanity publishing, all are equally valid tools to get your ideas out into the wide world.

SO WHY 'FILIGREE'S Rule'? Why 'Some authors deserve some publishers'?

I forced myself to write that mantra on a spring day in 2012, during a week of contrasts.

The man who was essentially my father-in-law had just died of a heart attack in the hospital.

I received an acceptance letter for my first novel, a space opera romance, from a respected erotic-romance small-press publisher (after being advised not to even query it to large commercial fantasy and science-fiction publishers because it was 'too queer').

I discovered that playing online whack-a-mole with trolls and naïve authors put me on the edge of a figurative, legal, (and literal) cliff. Stepping back from the edge meant realizing I wasn't cut out to be an eagle-eyed forensic researcher on a crusade to save people from themselves. The sooner I listened to my inner nihilist the better.

I hoped the two groups found and preyed upon each other: the predators and the staunchly clueless alike. Maybe they'd go down in flames and clear the field for more responsible people.

Over the next nine years I worked out a compromise between my inner researcher and inner nihilist. If I saw predatory and/or inept publishers, I ignored them until I saw them doing something obviously illegal. Then I reported them to the proper authorities.

If I saw obviously and willfully clueless authors begging for help online, I no longer went out of my way to hold their hands or do research for them, except in very limited and trustworthy cases.

Everyone else was on their own.

Yeah, that's callous.

How I got there, from wide-eyed, innocent, and happy industry cheerleader in 1987, is a story that probably can't ever be told in public. *But I know of what I speak.*

I just can't do much for chronically credulous writers who either can't or won't do their research in the proper order. If at all. We can't save some people from themselves.

I hate to see smart, literate, skilled, and humane writers being taken in by bad publishers, literary agents, editors, etc.

So I'm still collecting updates related to worst-practices publishing. This book is a sloppy attempt to gather all those sporadic blog posts into one place.

It's not going to be an easy read. But if one sentence keeps one author from committing themselves to crushing disappointment, financial ruin, or at least some wasted years of effort, my inner researcher will count it as Good Work.

The More Things Change

I apologize in advance.

This book is going to be a nasty, cynical read. It will make some people unhappy. However, if you are one of the millions of folks just now deciding you want to become a published writer, you should probably read it!

I AGONIZED FOR ALMOST a year about writing down Filigree's Rule.

It goes against my every fiber as a researcher, mentor, and former publishing newbie. So many people helped me over the past thirty-five years, that I feel as if I have a moral obligation to pass on that assistance.

I've been part of various internet conversations about writing and art since 1994. I have been Filigree on several writers' sites for over two decades. I would not be published today without the help of mentors who came before me, coaxed me over the depressing moments, put up with and diplomatically derailed my attacks of Golden Word Syndrome, and guided me through the mazes of the publishing industry.

If I'd actually started listening to them earlier, I would probably have been published a decade sooner. Thank you, gentlefolk.

For years I've been trying to pay forward that guidance, helping newer writers and artists over the same pitfalls that nearly swallowed me.

I'm selectively backing off that mandate as of now, regarding specific groups of writers, literary agents, and publishers. If I see writers, agents, and publishers revealing certain strategies, creeds, worldviews, and tendencies, I will step aside silently. I will offer no impediment to the three groups meeting up. To be blunt, I hope they drag each other down into acrimony and penury, and leave a more open playing field for the rest of us.

I am tired of reading writers' forums and seeing variations on the phrase 'researching agents and publishers is so HARD'.

Of seeing writers complain that they resent having to take a week or so to research basic publishing strategies. That it's so difficult, and so confusing, they're thinking of self-publishing or giving up.

Fine. Save yourself the time and money. Go start an Ebay or Etsy crafts or reselling business. The chances are good you'll earn more from it than from publishing.

Look at it another way. How long did it take you to write your book? To set up a new business? To buy a house? To adopt a child? To finish a dissertation?

I know careful people who spent *years* researching agents and publishers to find the right fit, to increase their chances of getting an offer of representation or publication. Or to learn the strategies behind different ways of successful self-publishing.

Skilled professionals in many other fields must do continual research and training to update their skills, and keep abreast of current developments in their business. It's called 'remaining employable'. Writers are in business for themselves. If they want to count it as more than a hobby, they have to behave more like business people.

Am I victim-shaming? Maybe. I genuinely feel for anyone jumping into the publishing pool right now, because it is big and confusing.

There are a lot of sharks out there pretending to be helpful fishing guides.

Whenever there's money to be made, some folks will sell their souls and 401K funds for a shortcut...and other people will be dreaming up scams to facilitate it. This is nothing new. Go research the Dutch Tulip craze, or the California Gold Rush. There are always con artists and easy marks.

This also won't help soothe the folks sitting on five hundred rejection letters from agents and publishers:

Publishing is so much better now than in 1987, when I wrote my first novel-length manuscript.

More opportunities exist. Gone are the days when many mass-market paperback authors could live for a year or two on the advances from one or two books. Yet now, authors who retain or regain control of their back catalogs can republish out-of-print works much more easily, earning them more precious 'long tail' earning power and new fans. There are more books being published now, for better or worse.

It's up to us to stand out from the crowd.

That is Marketing 101.

This book is not about marketing.

But it is about RESEARCH.

The internet simplified a lot of things. There's more information on publishing now, more places to find it, and more ways to rate its effectiveness and honesty. If a new writer can't manage basic internet search skills and a modicum of skepticism, or if they are so caught up in their own apparent exceptionalism they can't make objective decisions? Maybe they shouldn't be writing with the intent to publish.

Maybe it's not worth my time, or it's not my place to try saving them from themselves.

I'll pass on what assistance I can.

I'm not important enough in any particular industry for my detailed opinion to matter. No one sane is going to think that one sentence or a hundred from me makes that much difference in the world. All I hope to do is coax people to engage their own brains and make their own decisions.

What are my parameters? My criteria for deciding whether a publisher, agent, editor, or even another writer might be a risky business bet or collaborator?

Stay tuned!

Red Flag Checklist TL;dr

If you don't want to read a hundred pages or so of the gritty details, no problem.

Here's a quick checklist. Follow these steps to see if a publisher, agent, editor, etc. might be worth contacting about your manuscript:

1. Do they want you to pay them upfront for publishing, and again through commissions on your book sales? They're a vanity publisher or agent, and might not be your best option.

2. Do they have bad histories? Do some social media digging on them. Look them up on local court dockets and corporation lists in their area, and on the Better Business Bureau if they're in the US.

3. Do they use emotional appeals as 'a family business', 'making your dreams come true' or other feel-good phrases? Even if they mean well, they might be promising too much.

4. Do they pick too many fights online?

5. Do they pay their authors, editors, cover artists, media people, etc?

6. Do they behave professionally?

7. Do they treat all their clients with the best possible service?

These questions may not help you find *your* publisher, editor, or agent, but they can sort out the ones you might not want to do business with.

Services and Sales Information

B eing published used to be a lot harder than it is now. Most of us agree on that.

Online access has become both boon and bane for writers.

Email queries and online databases have opened up the formerly mysterious, laborious, and costly process of finding publishers and agents, querying them, and waiting for each answer through the postal system. With the click of a button, new writers can query a publisher or agent, submit a story, or even self-publish. In fact, there is so much stuff published, blogged about, or otherwise preserved online that we are awash in a sea of information.

Finding the 'good stuff' increasingly means relying on review services, social media gatekeepers, and other trusted sources. Easy access has possibly made us lazy. I am amazed that more people appear to spend more time researching prices and features on new automobiles, than on their potential publisher. The necessary research can be time-consuming, sometimes as much as writing the book in the first place.

Any writer intent on publishing for profit (or even just for personal satisfaction) should learn and use research skills: tracking down primary and secondary sources, following information trails, judging past performances, analyzing online presences, being skeptical, and being objective.

The information new writers need to protect themselves is already on the internet, across numerous sites.

Some online sites may appear to be less friendly at first, and present harsh lessons that we might not like to hear. So we may gravitate to kinder communities where other newbies are there to hold our hands and feed our egos as long as we return the favor. There's nothing wrong with that. Humans are social creatures. The friendships we make through supportive social media can be just as fulfilling as face-to-face contacts.

But that level of trust and acceptance can contain danger, as well. New writers crave positive reinforcement, but all too often that comes with a sales pitch as a price tag.

Your peers in the more-supportive groups might not know very much, either, and give you bad information.

Certain parts of the publishing world share startling similarities with multi-level marketing, for-profit colleges, and pyramid schemes. Many groups rely on a constant stream of new authors/members to make up their sales profits, advertising clicks, or general internet 'visibility'. Many show less real profit from their alleged businesses, than from recruiting and selling services to new members.

Many victims, no matter how victimized, can't accept the truth because it would mean that they got taken in. They already put in so much effort, they'll delude themselves into thinking 'This time it will work for me!'

This is often called 'The Sunk Cost Fallacy'.

The more self-aware victims think it means they are losers and fools, and remain silent out of shame and anger. They sometimes even accept those predatory parameters as 'the way publishing works', publish with other dubious publishers hoping 'this time it will be different', or even go on to found dubious publishing companies or literary agencies of their own—while earnestly believing they are doing good, because that is all they know.

Sometimes they know they're in with a bad crowd, and recruit newer writers to become part of an almost-Ponzi scheme. The earnings from new writers will help pay royalties for the publisher's first group of writers, leaving the newest ones exposed to the most financial loss if the publisher folds.

Publishers don't have to be actively villainous to be bad news for their authors.

Lots of new businesses over-commit or use up their capital investments within a couple of years. If the market is bad, or the publisher suffers a personal or family problem that requires more attention, the business can suffer. Learning which publishers have gone this route before, or might be going through it currently, might save authors untold stress and financial losses of their own.

The smartest, savviest people can be duped by the right pitch. Social engineering works. I know too many stage magicians and information security professionals to deny it.

Just because I am being selective about my online involvements and whistleblowing, doesn't mean I would arbitrarily cut off every well-meaning new writer. These are some of the sites that I have found to be good places to start, for researching publishers and literary agencies. It took me a while to gather all of these, but at least listing them will save other folks that time.

First, you can always try some basic Search Engine-Fu: on your favorite search engine type "(company name) publishing scam" and see what kind of hits you get. Duck Duck Go is a great alternative to major search engines, if you don't want to be easily tracked online.

Some Internet-ranking sites like Alexa.com allow you (for a price or a free trial, depending on current offers) to see any online company's global and local ranks, plus numbers of sites linking to them, by inserting their web address into the search area. Through Alexa's site checking feature, you can see 'big picture' data on the traffic generated to and from a publisher's website.

What does that mean to a writer? If your prospective publisher claims to sell more books through their website than they do through other online sales portals (like Amazon, Kobo, Barnes & Noble, Smashwords, etc.) and they have Alexa rankings in the high millions—they aren't attracting many visitors to their site.

So who's buying their books?

For Amazon sales specifically (print and Kindle), you can only track other people's books with difficulty. A current Amazon Sales Rank (which is NOT directly associated with a dollars-earned value!) can be seen in the book information section of the listing.

Only Amazon knows day-to-day what their hottest, fastest-selling books are, and they aren't going to easily release that information. That sales rank number does not track direct popularity, but rates-of-sale over short periods of time.

Very high number rankings (especially into the millions) indicate very low or slow sales. No Amazon ranking for a book? That means there hasn't been a single sale on Amazon, for that particular edition. Amazon isn't the only online sales portal, of course, and Sales Rank isn't perfectly representative for strong best-sellers.

From 2011 to 2015, my research and others' appeared to show that books with sales rank under 4 digits (1000-9000) were probably selling hundreds of copies a day.

A sales rank of 20,000-60,000 likely meant that book was selling dozens of copies a day.

Sales ranks of 100,000-200,000 might mean the book sold a few dozen copies a month.

Any sales rank over 1,000,000 seemed to indicate the book had only sold one or two copies in the last twelve months.

Is that still the case? I don't know. I don't work for Amazon.

But if you are a self-published author selling through Amazon's Kindle service, you can apply your sales rank to the performance of other people's books, and get a better picture.

Easiest thing to remember about sales ranks:

The lower the number, the higher rate of sales.

If you are already working in publishing, book-selling, education, or the library fields, you may have access to **Nielsen BookScan**, or know somebody who does. With BookScan data, you can look up the sales history of most print publications. BookScan may not cover all print sales of a specific book, but sales outlet participation is increasing rapidly.

Why care about your publisher's previous print sales? Why not believe their press releases and website advertising? You can see fairly accurate tracking of their books, which may give you an indication of your likely print sales. Believe me, all the major publishers and most small presses follow their competitors' BookScan numbers.

Check the publisher's current sales ranks on as many platforms as you can. See if their works are available through regional, national, and international distributors. If the publisher has multiple pages of strongly-selling books across a couple of big vendor platforms, they're probably doing something right.

RE: Amazon. Here's a tip I have sadly learned firsthand. Look at *all* of a publisher's book ranks on Amazon. Or if they are prolific, at least the first 10 pages (30 to 50 titles). If most of those books are ranked 600,000 to over 1,000,000, but a few of them are are between 150,000 and 300,000...look out.

As far as any outsider can tell, Amazon sales ranks of very slow-selling books can shoot up dramatically with single sales. Watch them the next day, and see where those books are then. If the ranks are still in lower-digit sales rank territory, they might be steady sellers. If they've already slid 50,000 to 100,000 points, then you are looking at the aftermath of an isolated sale.

If you see a lot of those high-number sales ranks, it can indicate a publisher who can't market effectively.

Sales ranks can also help self-published authors zero in on similar books and how well their cover design, cover art, blurbs, and other marketing tools might be helping sales. Learn from them, but try not to obviously copy.

THESE ARE BASIC RESEARCH tools, most of which are available for free to anyone with an internet connection and a working knowledge of English. Bear in mind that all of these sources are subject to change, and might not remain at the addresses I have listed.

Some other places to start your online research:

'Making Light', the blog of Teresa and Patrick Nielsen Hayden, Avram Grumer, Jim MacDonald, and Abi Sutherland. A wide-ranging and informed discussion of many publishing topics, from professionals with many years in the field: *https://nielsenhayden.com/makinglight/*

You can find some information about how to spot scam publishers, agents, and workshops over at *Reedsy.com*. Caveat Emptor: Reedsy's not immune to the creeping rot of vanity publishing or its emotionally-charged code languages. I applaud their attention on the worst offenders, though.

Writer Beware is the SFWA (Science Fiction Writers of America) public branch of their Committee on Writing Scams, which deals not only with 'issues that affect professional authors, but with the problems and pitfalls that face aspiring writers.'

https://www.sfwa.org/for-authors/writer-beware/

AbsoluteWrite is an online writing industry site with 40,000+ members at varying professional levels, discussing topics across the publishing and creative industries. When they get their new servers up and running, go look for *https://absolutewrite.com/*

Disclaimer: though I am an eleven-year member of AbsoluteWrite, I don't get kickbacks financial or intangible from their site. And I've had my own nose smacked (deservedly so) by the AbsoluteWriter moderators more than once.

A word about the sites mentioned above: shady publishers and agents *hate* them.

So if you run into a publisher, agent, or author who complains about Making Light, Writer Beware, or AbsoluteWrite, give those people a second and third look before doing business with them.

To get a glimpse of what agents are seeking and selling, try looking them up on QueryTracker *https://querytracker.net*

Some more-current literary agent and editor news can be found at Manuscript Wish List *https://www.manuscriptwishlist.com/*

PROBLEMATIC PUBLISHERS AND AGENTS

This section looks at warning signals, risky behavior, outright red flags, and the problems that clueless or predatory publishers and literary agents can cause authors.

My Criteria for Shady Stuff

I have a long list of things that usually lead me to invoke Filigree's Rule against a publisher, literary agent, editor, author, etc.

This list will infuriate some people, because it's not politically correct by any measure. But it accurately reflects my experiences and observations in publishing over at least the last two decades. It's also inspired by the actual online or in-person gaffes I've seen from actual companies and individuals. Nor are they publishing-specific: many of the same factors show up in multi-level marketing, the art world, for-profit education, and other businesses.

To recap, here's the rule: *Some authors deserve some publishers, and vice versa, and I will not stand in their way.*

Publishing is an odd game no matter what variety an author chooses: true self-publishing, commercial trade publishing, a hybrid mix of the two. But there is now a lot of solid information about publishing available online or at a public library, for anyone with basic reading skills. If writers can't manage that, then they're probably not publishable authors...yet.

I can hear some of you saying: "But Filigree, if your standards are this high, it's impossible to get published!"

No, it's not.

It's really easy to get published *badly*, and suffer the consequences for years. At its most spectacularly-terrible levels, getting publishing badly can tank your writing career, your love of writing, and your self-worth.

I have stories in commercially-published royalty-paying anthologies, several self-published novels, and I was a small-press author for nine years (with publishers who took no money from me and promptly paid me royalties on sales). In the last 34 years I've had two literary agents and interned for another. I've written art-related grants and created effective marketing copy for luxury online sales platforms. I'm also one of the laziest and least-organized fiction writers I know, and I got published.

High standards protect you, your work, your self-respect, your bank account, and your legacy.

So, on to the list of Publishing Fails. One entry here isn't always a guaranteed 'caution', but multiples are. The first entry is probably the most important. If you do nothing else, learn how to ask and answer this one...

Is This A Vanity Publisher?

Does the publisher make most of its money from its authors—through publishing fees, reading fees, marketing packages, book buying requirements for authors, or any other scheme—instead of from actual sales to wider markets?

How do you tell a vanity publisher from a commercial publisher?

If the publisher asks the author for money upfront (and beyond its contracted after-market cut of sales) at any stage in the process, *it is a vanity publisher.*

A commercial publisher will pay you an upfront advance for the rights to publish your book. If they don't pay advances, they will be clear that they expect to make their money off sales, after publication. *They won't ask for money upfront from you.*

Does the publisher refer to its commercial trade-publisher rivals as 'legacy' publishers? That's a derogatory term popularized among self-published authors who, rightly or wrongly, feel that commercial publishing has betrayed or ignored them. When other publishers use the 'legacy' term, be wary. It might herald a vanity publisher.

Does the publisher say that it doesn't accept every mms sent to it, therefore it is not a vanity publisher? Wrong. Not how it works. Even major vanity publishers have rejected works (though usually from authors they think are going to be 'difficult' about paying them, or throwing snits about their lack of editing, marketing, etc.)

Does the publisher insist that the author's payment is only a small fraction of the actual cost of publication? Given the lack of 'publishing' work that goes into the usual vanity-published mms, an author's $2000, $3600, or $5000 'subsidy' is probably far more than what the publisher will spend on the book.

Did you know that the average small-press editor often gets only $50-$100 to edit an 80,000 to 95,000-word manuscript? Or they're offered a share of royalty income instead?

Remember, you can often 'see' a book's sales rank on Amazon and other publishing platforms. Will a book with only a few sales a year make enough in royalties to pay you and an editor?

Any money made after that 'author investment', through outside sales or author purchases, is just gravy to the vanity publisher. They're often soaking most of their authors several times: the initial publishing 'fee' the author paid, 'marketing packages' paid by the author, and the publisher's commission on sales.

Does the publisher call themselves a 'hybrid publisher' or 'subsidy publisher'? Watch out. That does not mean the same thing as a hybrid author (an author who has both published commercially and self-published.) 'Hybrid' publishers often claim they offer advance-paid contracts to authors they think are more worthy or marketable, while reserving author-paid subsidy contracts for works which might be riskier in the market. They are essentially saying to the latter author, "Oh, we don't believe in your work enough to fund its publication ourselves. But we'll happily take your money and claim a percentage of sales later, if you pay us to publish it for you."

By the way, vanity publishers hate being called vanity publishers. That's why they invented the term 'subsidy' or 'partnership' publisher', and hide behind the (often very rare) advance-paid contract. Legally, they can say: "We do commercial, advance-paying publication, just look at this handful of authors!" while drawing attention away from the hundreds or thousands of authors who paid to be published.

Another favorite gambit of vanity publishers is to claim they offer a full refund of the author's 'investment' once that book reaches a certain number or dollar amount of sales. All the while knowing that earn-out will be nearly impossible unless the author buys all those books.

Usually at highly-inflated prices, too.

There is nothing wrong with paying a printing service to self-publish a hard-copy or three hundred of your magnum opus. But make sure the printer is clear about their role: they will only do the background work on the thing, and you the author are responsible for selling the product.

Authors Starting Their Own Publishing Company

Is this a vanity publisher founded by an author who was previously disappointed by one or more other vanity publishers, and now thinks they know how to do it 'better'? Whether they are predators seeing an easy market or genuinely well-meaning but ignorant publishers...avoid, avoid, avoid.

These can be plague carriers of misinformation and bad practices. They may start with noble intentions. Temptation often looms when they realize they can make more money selling services to authors than in selling books. While still taking a tidy cut of the small income from real sales.

Likewise, if those authors tried the commercial trade-publishing route query after query, and never got anywhere, they really don't have any background to help them start a new royalty-paying publishing company.

A very few successful publishers have started out that way, and they have some things in common: they had a background in the business, enough industry contacts, and enough funding to survive the first years of business. They are usually very selective in the other authors they sign on.

Local Interest and Vanity Publishing

The vanity publishing industry has taken a beating the last few years, due to bad publicity and the ease of digital self publishing. But there are still plenty of suckers out there who are uninformed, lazy, or paranoid enough to make easy prey for the remaining vanity publishers.

Unlike self-publishing where an author contracts out to separate professionals for editing, cover design, formatting, marketing, etc, vanity publishers claim to do it all for you (often at abysmal quality and high prices).

Unlike book printers, which merely print and bind (or format, for e-books), vanity publishers often promise that they will sell the book, too. More and more of them are adding language to their front matter telling authors to be responsible for selling their own books...but the vanities cheerfully pay themselves a part of any sales off their website or other online platforms. Even after charging the author for publication!

If a publisher takes part of a book's sales price, the publisher should be doing something to earn it. Most vanity publishers do not, but they are excellent at creating a cultlike us-against-them mentality in their authors, to keep those authors on the hook for paying for more books (and bringing in other authors). They'll even brand themselves as self-publishers or 'assisted self publishers' just to further confuse authors.

Beware of writer's magazines like Writer's Digest, which in the last decades have become ridden with vanity publishing ads. Be cautious of popular magazines, late-night television, and other programming aimed at consumers (elderly, ultra-religious, unemployed or under-employed, blue collar workers) that might be receptive to vanity publishing, because the vanities are advertising there, too.

Beware of advertising hooks like: 'Have you written a book?' or 'Do you want to be a published author?' I've seen major vanity publishers show up at local and regional book festivals, to hook unwary authors.

Several years ago I found another venue for vanity publishing advertising: local-interest neighborhood newspapers. It makes a sick kind of sense.

There on page 38 of my own local newspaper was a decent-sized ad for Dorrance. There's a lot about Dorrance online, and they are not the only vanity publisher trolling for victims in media advertising and local-interest features.

Local news is always hungry for feel-good stories about their citizens publishing books. Some examples just from my little suburban paper over the last few years: grieving widows and parents celebrating their lost loved ones with a published memoir, people recovering from dire illness or injury writing about their ordeal and triumph, would-be self-help gurus offering their tactics for success (the professional self-improvement folks almost always self-publish), senior citizens recounting family histories, people of faith giving testament to their deeply held beliefs, and teens writing fantasy and science fiction epics.

Many of these are vanity published, because the authors didn't know enough to research the difference between commercial (where the publisher pays the author) and self publishing, but did a cursory search for publishing. Or the authors were recruited by a vanity publisher.

Many local-interest newspaper staffers don't know better, either, and wouldn't care if they did. They don't have the time or the skill to research which feel-good story comes from a commercially-published author, a self-pub author, or a vanity-published victim.

I fired off a letter to the editor, and the next week the offending ad was gone. But I have no idea if that was due to my letter, or that the publisher's ad run had simply ended. That same paper, in the years since this example, has offered dozens of 'Local Author!' stories, with about 80% of them being vanity-published.

How Long Have They Been In Business?

Publishing, for better or worse, is not an entry level business. Without experience and capital to shield the first two-to-five years of operations, many small publishers quickly flare out or thud to the ground.

Any authors taking that ride with them can find publishing rights tied up for years, if the matter goes through bankruptcy court and creditors. Authors are nearly always far down the list of approved creditors getting a share of the bankruptcy proceeds!

So if you are looking at a new publisher under two or three years in business, consider only committing work to them that you can afford to lose, or accept that it might be a low-earning project. I'm not knocking 'labors of love' if the publisher is a dear friend, but be realistic.

The new publisher has to show that its owners know what they're doing, they have a solid five-year-plan in place for their business, and have some kind of funding in place for the lean times.

Likewise, take a clear look at your own timeframe and expectations.

Most authors are not going to get rich in this business.

Most authors are not going *to get rich right away* in this business, but a comfortable income can be built over time.

If you want instant income, or if a publisher seems to promise this to you, please calm down and think again (and keep your day job!)

Your Publishing Dreams Come True!

Does the publisher's, agent's, etc. website or brochure say anything resembling these phrases:

"We're here to make your publishing dreams come true."

"Traditional legacy publishers won't take unknown authors."

"We are not a vanity publisher because we don't publish everything submitted to us."

"We are a partnership publisher."

"Authors are their own best sales force."

Those are important key phrases that often involve misinformation and outright deception. Moreover, responsible publishers rarely make those claims.

They're not there for your dreams, but their profit. Good publishers will get a kick out of having happy, loyal authors, because it's just sound marketing these days. But in the end, publishing decisions are based on cold hard ROI extrapolations. For non-marketing people, ROI means 'Return On Investment'.

You know...capitalism.

As for 'Traditional' or Legacy' publishing? Those are attempted slurs mostly used by vanity publishers, some small presses, and many self-published authors who picked them up with other bad habits.

'Trade publishers' sell books; no one with any real background in the publishing world is going to call themselves a 'traditional' publisher. It's most often an insult leveled at trade publishers by outsiders. So that phrase can often be a sign to a new author: be careful about picking a publisher who uses those terms to describe other publishers!

Commercial publishers love finding debut, unknown authors if those authors have viable books that can be easily marketed to valuable readerships. They love it so much that in the romance, fantasy, science fiction, and mystery fields, midlist authors often need to rebrand with a new pen-name to recapture some of that debut magic.

The core definition of vanity publishing doesn't involve taking on every project.

Just those whose authors can either make the publisher enough money to justify a 'royalty' contract.

Or those who can be counted on to hand over thousands of dollars for 'partnership' contracts, as well as a majority of published book sales earnings.

Royalty rates vary. In small-press and vanity publishers offering 'value added' services, I've seen everything from 75/25% splits between publisher and author, down to 50/50%. The publisher is usually going to get the largest share.

Authors can be effective sales people for their own work, but their primary job should be writing more books. If any publisher appears to claim its authors must do the largest percentage of promoting their own books (or even help promote other authors in the company), then why on earth is the author paying the publisher commission income on every sale?

Press-releases? Those can sent out for free, from certain bundling services, and hardly anyone useful to book sales reads them.

Covers? Have you seen most vanity-published covers? Compare them with similar genre or theme novels from bigger commercial publishers? Is that cover, editing, and desultory 'marketing' worth not only an often $2000 or more upfront fee and 50 to 75% commission on individual sales going to the publisher?

Editing? Does the publisher pay upfront for the services of editors, cover artists, book designers, etc? Does it pay them on a royalty basis?

With the latter method, the production team makes money when the book sells. The more sales, the more the team earns. This sounds enticing in theory, but not every book is going to have amazing sales. (I've heard from multiple editors who've worked for now-defunct or fading publishers. These editors cited making as little as $25 per novel-length editing job, or less.) In some cases, only content/development editors were paid by royalty; the line editors were offered copies as payment!

Some publishers will offer their editors a small base salary, plus royalty commissions. Some offer nothing but the royalty.

Small digital publishers seem to be the most prone toward this arrangement. They often sell it as 'a way to gain experience' or 'we must all make sacrifices to make this company great'. Often the royalty-only policy goes along with the company's misuse of intern services, which are strictly limited under different countries' laws.

New, relatively inexperienced production staff will often agree to the royalty-only payment system to get their foot in the door.

But if sales are too low, competent editors get fed up and leave, leading to new or lesser-skilled editors doing less-competent work, which leads in turn to lower and lower sales. At the same time, a company so underfunded it has to delay paying some of its most critical workers, may have other cash-flow problems as well. They may not be able to afford strong or timely advertising, for example.

Going only by my two decades of watching the publishing industry, a royalty-only arrangement for production staff doesn't inspire my complete confidence in a publisher. I won't say 'no' just for that, but it is a warning sign that makes me dig deeper to find other problems.

Ask these things of any publisher. It's their job to have an honest answer. It's okay to ask your prospective publisher how it pays its editors. If they avoid answering or get angry, that's another big red flag for you.

Is This A Faith-Based Publisher?

Alert: more political incorrectness ahead!

Is the publisher, author, literary agent, etc. a vocal and active member of any fundamentalist religion (not limited to Christianity)?

If so, their legitimate publishing efforts may be focused tightly on witnessing for that faith, and less on reaching a neutral audience outside it.

If you are writing material that doesn't fit their mandate, you and they might not be comfortable partners. Don't push to join their club 'to make them change', or whatever your social agenda may be. Leave the churchfolk in peace, and find a club where you and your work are more welcome.

In some cases, the publisher, etc. may be using religion as a smokescreen and a lure to attempt *affinity fraud* against sympathetic clients. Until the clients realize they've been had, there is no point in trying to pierce the cloud of dogma and secret-handshake code words. The victims will only see you as the enemy trying to lead them astray.

See my Case Study about Tate Publishing, later on in this book, for one (infamous) example of a 'faith-based' publisher misusing its authors' honest faith and belief.

Likewise, is the publisher, author, agent, etc. a vocal and active advocate of certain fringe cultural beliefs? This can include but is not limited to: Flat Earthers, Intelligent Design, Climate Change Deniers, New World Order conspiracy theorists, White Supremacists, UFO enthusiasts, Qanon, and certain New Age healing/lifestyle proponents.

They may be literate, intelligent, and a helluva lot of fun in discussions—but a publishing business arrangement might be risky. They can abruptly lash out at you if you don't follow them and their worldview. Is their brand your brand? Because it will be, if you are associated with them.

Spot Unprofessional Behavior

Does the publisher, author, agent, etc. engage in long, defensive, and generally ineffective rants online, when faced with any criticism of their business? This may also be Nature's way of saying 'Do not touch' to the rest of us.

Likewise, if the publisher, etc. has a lot of overtly threatening legal copy about defamation, ownership, and Non-Disclosure Agreements (NDAs) on their website or online comment signatures; or makes out-of-proportion legal threats in response to online criticism.

If a publisher, etc. appears to have a history of making legal threats, consult the court system in their physical locality to discover if they've actually initiated legal proceedings against detractors, unhappy authors, and/or business competition. Many less than-scrupulous publishers, etc. attempt to scare their authors into silence with contractual agreements barring the latter from any sort of public 'defamation'. Whenever I see legal disclaimers and threats that are too strident, I know to ignore that company.

Try to research the locations in which a publisher or literary agency has set up their 'official' incorporation documents. If it's not in the city or state in which they actually reside/do business in (even in the Covid work-from-home era), research why. Sometimes that can mean concealing a location to avoid potential client stalking or even lawsuits, and sometimes it can indicate outright fraud.

I've seen several cases in which very deceptive 'publishers' claimed workspaces at mail-drop addresses, run-down motels, or industrial park locations where not even a Better Business Bureau search could find the actual office.

WHEN ASKED ABOUT ANY of this stuff, does the publisher or agent lash out and use an author's doubts and questions as an excuse to withdraw the publication offer, or harass and belittle the author?

Does the agent, publisher, workshop manager, etc. directly confront their clients or skeptics with threatening emails or social media posts? Or send minions or makes up sock puppet online accounts to do this. That's now one of my strongest reasons for ignoring any publishing professional, the moment I see them engage in such bad behavior.

Sock puppets are a feature of the Internet. They're going to surface. But if you do a little research, you might find a publisher/author has their own name, a writing alias, and two or three made-up 'friends' or 'reviewers'. All of whom are busy writing 5-star reviews and calling down the wrath of God on dissenting comments.

Many times these stunts come from the young and clueless, but age is no guarantee of innocent well-meaning enthusiasm.

Around 2016, a 19-year-old self-described wunderkind writer/blogger/(and yes) publisher was caught red-handed trying to claim she was an employee of Penguin Books, in order to work an elaborate scheme to get copies of her self-published (not by Penguin) book in front of reputable reviewers. She also claimed job and internship credits that she didn't earn. Her self-publishing 'press' was at the time still actively courting more young and clueless bloggers/writers (with an upper age limit of 30 in her help-wanted page).

There's a long-running case from the UK, where a well-known thriller author boasted in public at a 2012 writing convention of using multiple sock-puppets to feed and even discuss reviews of his books. What's worse, he's used the same technique to troll other authors, to the point where his publisher is now 'looking into the matter'. (I'm not giving him any links because he's more arrogant than entertaining. You can find him with basic SearchFu.) Why he did this, I have no idea. His writing is good enough to stand alone.

Note: sock-puppets are different from pen-names. Pen-names (pseudonyms) are often chosen to either re-brand an author's new and different work, or to protect an author from career and/or family-ruining public scrutiny. The only true privacy on the Internet is on the Dark Web, via an onion browser. Out here in the sampled, logged, and cataloged web, it's not that hard to figure out who people are.

Sock-puppets created to spread misinformation or to counter bad publicity almost always break down under scrutiny. You should probably not pick a publisher or agent who indulges in that kind of behavior. Don't associate with writers who do this, lest you end up sharing their bad rep. If nothing else, it's a waste of their time and yours.

FOR EMPHASIS: DOES the author, publisher, or agent publicly engage in online fights over bad reviews? Over good reviews that were not quite gushingly positive enough?

That's sloppy business practice.

Reviews are for readers.

Even horrible one-star reviews may reveal something that other readers may like, leading them to buy the book. I've bought books that had one-star reviews, because I felt that the reviewer's comment proved they were clueless idiots. I've had readers buy my books based on poor reviews, for the same reason. The worst one-star review may actually be better for a book than the blandest or most effusive 5-star review. Especially if the latter comes across as fake.

Does the publisher make use of paid You-Tube 'testimonials' to pitch its authors' books? Be wary: sometimes these are legit, but recorded by authors still in their happy honeymoon phase with a bad publisher. Sometimes, those testimonials are fake from the start.

Does the publisher have no idea that paid reviews (Fiverr, Craigslist, etc.) are the kiss of death to a legitimate book, and may backfire? Amazon has been cracking down on these fake testimonials lately, but with mixed results. Remember: Amazon makes money on those fake reviews, too.

A related issue that may not directly harm authors: publishers airing their organizational dirty laundry and internal spats in public, via social media and lawsuits. For me, this always hints at a publisher's potential instability and overreaction to criticism (internal or external). I'm always calculating how much of the publisher's capital will end up paying for the lawsuit...and why was it triggered in the first place?

At least one fairly reputable literary agency closed its doors in 2020, due to the founding agents' inflammatory online comments regarding Black Lives Matter protests. In solidarity with BLM, many of their junior agents quit. At least one more agency was gutted and forced to hire all-new staff except for the lead agent. (I would be very leery about querying those new agents, myself, based solely on their association with this agent.)

At the very least, internal disagreements made public can show how a publisher has written its founding partnership contracts. If they can't amicably resolve their partnership disagreements in private through counsel and arbitration...what the hell are they going to do with authors who have serious problems with them?

It's also a sobering reminder to the rest of us: if you're going into business with friends and family, protect everyone involved with solid, precisely-written contracts from the start.

How amenable is the publisher or literary agency to changing its contract? Is a problematic clause there because the business owner honestly didn't know better, or is there an ulterior motive? Does the publisher or agent react with instant and over-the-top anger at any questions about their contract terms?

A case in point with the serial numbers filed off: multiple authors engaged with a small press to publish a themed anthology. One author noted that the contract was written to pay authors last, after every other publisher expense was paid. If the publisher had said: 'This is the only way we can afford to publish', it would have sucked but been honest. Generally, this kind of *net payment* often results in lower amounts to authors, and can be used to winnow out all possible profits before paying authors.

Instead, the publisher veiled its language with promises that 'authors will make more money on royalties this way'. *Which, if they were making that much money, they could afford to pay their authors off gross sales, not net.* When asked to clarify this issue, the business owner threw a tantrum and decided the author was insulting the way the publisher did business.

Hint: that's not an insult, that's a well-meaning question. But there is a cultural response (found in many cultures, alas) that the best way to answer a moral, ethical, or challenging business question is to go on the offensive not only with denials, but accusations of the other party being guilty of the same or worse. Watch for that type of 'projection' behavior: it might be the first clue you have about a future publisher or literary agent meltdown!

At the very least, do you want this fight every time you have an honest question?

Sloppy Work and Previous Failures

Does the publisher, author, agent, etc. show large numbers of errors in their website, promotional material, or online social media posts? In their published books?

Do they show a lack of cross-cultural knowledge when talking to authors (for example, not knowing how dates are written in British vs. American usage?) Are these errors obvious, chronic, and wide-ranging?

When called on it, do the individuals insist that 'social media isn't real business, so accuracy doesn't matter there'?

A smart, experienced publisher, agent, or editor tries to present themselves as professional all the time.

Does the publisher, agent, etc. have a verifiable track record in their field?

Publishing is not an entry-level position.

Most publishing professionals will have solid backgrounds in or closely related to their field. If not, consider this: would you trust a brain surgeon who can't prove she knows what she's doing? Why should you trust a brand new, unknown publisher?

Likewise, check around to learn if the publisher/owner has a long list of failed publications, imprints, or publishing 'houses', one after another. Too many of those can indicate unprofessional behavior and a tendency to bail out rather than fix problems.

Concerning agents: even if you like the literary agent, is the agency itself suspect in any way?

I won't name them, but there are some agencies that break my heart whenever I see them mentioned online. They have agents I would query in a caffeine-fueled heartbeat...if they were not working for or had been mentored by those firms. There's too much online doubt and too many bad stories about the founders or other agents there, for me to take a chance on those shiny enticing agents. It sucks, but that's what background checks can show. Better know this stuff before you query, than after you've been published and are in a hellish professional death spiral.

This should be so basic that it shouldn't need saying: Does the agent charge their authors for representation?

Some agents do charge a modest fee for office supplies, but that's usually added to their commission. Standard business practice is that agents only get paid off book and rights sales...so they have a vested interest in selling manuscripts for the best possible return.

If you run into an agent who does charge hefty fees, stop and think: if I pay this person, what incentive do they have for selling my book? It's the same equation as vanity publishers.

I know an AbsoluteWrite thread about a literary agency that was allegedly charging big fees.

I'm including a quote here, because the fees claimed are so egregious. I've removed the agent name myself:

<*The following is a direct quote from a mass email sent out by [**agent name redacted**] to clients and former clients. Let authors beware!*

"In the new contract, for any new Work(s) there will be an administrative fee of five hundred dollars ($500.00), made payable to the Agency upon signing. This is a one-time fee, unless the Work(s) do not contract with a publisher and require renewing after one year. Renewals are two hundred

fifty dollars ($250.00) per year. Upon publication of the Work(s), only the LLA 15% shall apply.">

It's telling that the agency's 'defense' fell back on some of questionable tactics I've mentioned earlier, including the use of 'Christian' dogwhistle speech often associated with affinity fraud.

Family Business Danger Signs

S till more politically-incorrect stuff. Is the publisher, agent, editor, or other service provider running a very small, family-owned or single proprietor shop?

If so, they may be vulnerable to losing the business after sickness or disaster.

Before doing business with such individuals, check their social media presence for indications of chronic illness, family problems, or multiple past bankruptcies or business failures, failed Kickstarter programs, etc. This could be a danger sign for the future, if the business owners have not laid out contingency plans. Double danger warning if the publisher, etc. has used health, financial, and/or family emergencies in the past as multiple excuses for not meeting contractual goals.

It's heartbreaking.

Some of the nicest, most talented, and well-meaning people can get caught up in financial nightmarcs.

But unless you are family, those aren't your nightmares. You're just the writer. Not the therapist, not the enabler, not the venture capitalist. Walk away when you smell trouble, unless you are fully willing to invest not only your story and money, but possibly your sanity in this business venture.

Does the publisher, author, agent, etc. show strong indications (in their social media, public appearances, or published material) of a serious neurochemical disorder or physical brain injury? Don't go there unless you are a trained, licensed medical professional or caregiver doing your job. Unless there are other, less damaged people involved, this is probably not a good business risk for you.

Especially when authors are seeking agents: is the agent a trainwreck? Financially, medically, or emotionally? Check their social media. Newer junior agents tend to share a lot on social media, and if they are in dire economic or mental health straits, chances are you'll hear about it.

Why should you as an author be wary of these agents? Why not give them a chance? Because younger, unestablished agents are themselves on probation with their agencies and their profession. It's hard work and it generally doesn't pay well at the start. Lots of newer agents leave the field...often leaving their authors in the lurch.

If you see hints that an agent might not stay in the business, reconsider querying them in the first place.

You will notice that many seasoned literary agents don't overshare on social media. There's a reason.

My next point pains me to write it, but I have to. It's a real problem.

Does the agent or publishing company owner excuse their sloppy writing, editing, or business practices because of neurodiverse issues such as (but not limited to) dyslexia or being on the autism spectrum?

This is a touchy one, because I'm on the spectrum and I have neurodiverse friends. But they are high-functioning within their spectrum and they manage to understand and apply various literary, academic, and scientific style manuals with no problem.

I saw this recently with several people who were in the position to charge money for various writing services. They claimed to be 'shut out' of agent representation or mainstream publishing because of their neurodiversity and attendant writing quirks.

Upon further examination of sample materials online, those proved to be not so much as 'quirks', but simply awkward writing that could have used serious structural and line editing.

These folks were not being professional.

Their neurodiversity may also come as a package with some other negative issues and life events: they may just be at a really bad point, and possibly unable to help themselves, much less you as a client or author.

Can they be stable, effective professional business partners, or not?

This is especially important when considering potential literary agents, editors, or critique/writing partners.

It's no damn fair that neurotypicals rule the publishing world, and that diverse individuals *for many reasons* must fight even harder for representation and respect. It's admirable for someone to fight the good fight for their own work. But when they hang up a shingle and advertise for clients, they need to be as professional and responsible as possible.

Otherwise, the aforementioned claims come across not as sympathetic, but as whiny. Given the choice between an editor who shows as skilled, professional, and interesting, or one who blames the rigged system for their sloppy work...guess who I'm hiring?

There are many neurodiverse writers, artists, bloggers, (and yes) even agents and editors out there who've hammered out a place of respect for themselves and their work.

Social Media Platforms

Even if this isn't a vanity publisher, does the publisher insist a fiction author have a strong, well-developed social media presence as a firm condition of being accepted for publication?

Does the agent insist that social media fame is a strong part of their consideration to represent you as a client?

Agents generally ask this to gauge if a nonfiction author has a large online following that can be recruited for promo (because many publishers want this, too.) Agents don't generally do marketing or promo, but your author platform & fanbase can help them attract publishers. If you don't have that, it shouldn't be a deal breaker...as long as you have a great book.

It shouldn't be a problem at all, if you're writing fiction.

Does the publisher use language mandating the author's self-promotion as the bulk of a book's marketing? Ask the publisher what marketing of their own are they planning to use, to justify their cut of sales. Or walk away. Those kinds of contract stipulations often indicate publishers who already know they can't effectively market outside their own author contact list.

If the author's social media platform is going to be utilized alongside publisher efforts, then yay for everybody. If it looks like the author does most of the work...nope.

I recently read an online post where a new author talked about her publisher sending her a 150-page PDF booklet on marketing, including the (paraphrased) advice: 'hang out and comment on influential blogs in your genre, in hopes of scoring a review of your own work.' Now, I do not know the publisher, nor have I seen what other nuggets of wisdom are in the PDF, but I can guess what their sales are likely to be. Unless the publisher is also jumping through flaming hoops to reach distributors and high-ranking review sites. And if they're sending the equivalent of a marketing course textbook to their authors, it's likely they won't be doing their share in the first place.

Does the publisher insist that its authors spend time on social media (or even at brick-and-mortar stores) promoting not only the author's books, but those from other authors with the publisher?

Hint: that's what marketing departments do.

Even worse, does the publisher strongly suggest or outright ask the author to buy as many books as possible from other authors with that publisher? That can be an indication of a publisher desperately trying to push its sales numbers higher.

So again, how do they justify taking a 50 to 75% share of book sales?

How Many Genres Are They Publishing?

Is a new/small publisher, agent, etc. narrowly focused on a couple of writing genres, or do they appear to accept many genre categories?

If the latter applies, the company may be flinging projects at the wall and waiting to see what sticks. They may not have the in-depth knowledge and industry relationships to be an effective player in all their genres. For genre-focused publishers in the romance, horror, and SFF fields, make sure these companies are aware of and attend at least some of the major or regional conventions devoted to those genres.

If they've been around for more than two years and they're still a small publisher—and still behaving this way—then they're just farting around. They may not be a vanity publisher, but they're probably more committed to making many tiny sales off many authors, than large sales off a few authors. The long tail marketing pattern (small profits but many sales over a long period of time) works well for publishers who keep their production and marketing overhead low, but not great for authors who are making single to double-digit sales per year, per book.

Is the publisher expanding too fast, into too many genres and imprints, without solid plans to equally promote each one?

Are they opening 'preferred' imprints to specific groups of authors, with better royalty terms and marketing, but leaving the rest to flounder?

What Rights Does A Publisher Claim?

Does the publisher demand publishing rights for which it is not trained or prepared to exercise right away?

Many small presses are using some variant of this language: 'Technology is changing so fast that we want to lock down rights we can't use just yet, but may in the future'.

No, just no.

Technology changes all the time. A publisher has to be willing to adapt. But they also have to prove they are able to use those rights promptly. At the time of contract signing, the publisher needs to be able to show the author concrete, respectable proof of successful negotiations for audio, film, digital, foreign, and any other rights they may wish to claim on your book. Right then. Not some unknowable point down the line. If they haven't sold a book to a movie studio for a real treatment (not an option), they don't get that right for your book.

Regarding options:

Small presses, vanity presses, and some dicey agencies trumpet this or that Hollywood option on a book. Doesn't mean a thing until that option turns into a real script or better yet, a movie, or television/ streaming service show that outlasts its pilot episode.

Some options are respectable money for authors. Some are just a few hundred bucks. Knowing who paid the option is probably more important: if it's a studio, service, or director you've heard of, the associated publisher might be able to do right by you.

Be wary of publishers (often magazines or display sites) who hide exclusivity rights in their fine print. Paraphrasing from a recent Twitter discussion:

"Found a publisher saying at time of submission you are granting them all rights to the entry and the right to independently CREATE DERIVATIVE WORKS and publish IN PERPETUITY."

By merely submitting an entry to this publisher, the author is signing away all future rights to the work or its derivative works. I see this in some art and photo contests, but there the prizes are lucrative enough that artists might be willing to 'give up' their art.

Does the Publisher Dislike Agents?

Does the publisher refuse to deal with literary agents or other authors' representatives, and prefer to make contract arrangements solely with authors?

Does the publisher cast literary agents and other representatives in a negative light, as 'gatekeepers' and 'middlemen' at best, and outright crooks at worst? Does the publisher claim that, by insisting against agent involvement, they are helping authors keep more of their royalties? Is this a new publisher?

If 'yes' applies to most or all of these questions, some caution and further research may be in order.

Authors need to understand that skilled agents do far more than negotiate contracts and take commissions. At some point in an author's career, *rights* could be just as or more important than straight-up royalties on individual sales.

Unless an author is extremely well-informed, they might miss crucial details in rights management.

Some relevant examples: George Lucas was one of the first film directors to see the potential of merchandising and image licensing. Ergo, 'Star Wars' made ridiculous amount of money in merchandise. George R. R. Martin has creative control clauses in his contracts, meaning he gets to guide film and multi-media adaptations of his work.

If the agent or publisher isn't careful about rights sales, it can lead to derivative works that the author hates...or that even damage the author's career and reputation.

Some well-meaning publishers might encourage authors to consult a contract lawyer—not the same animal as a literary agent. Lawyers without publishing industry experience can be useless for and possibly detrimental to author/publisher contract negotiations. Lawyers with publishing industry experience are still generally not literary agents.

Even if they're well-meaning and have only their authors' financial gain in mind, publishers who exclude literary agents from negotiations may be shortchanging their authors in the long run. Of course, it's up to each author to do their research and weigh consequences.

More than that, a publisher who refuses to deal with agents may be revealing how little they know about publishing...or that they already know their contracts *do not favor the author.*

At least one very well known genre publishing imprint was founded by a person who said (I paraphrase): "Any author who negotiates a publishing contract without an agent involved...deserves what they get." Scuttlebutt, past history, and the publisher's core values suggest it may well have taken advantage of some unagented writers. Note: it's still a great publisher, and very respected, with a lot of satisfied authors.

How Are Their Book Covers?

Does the publisher allow authors to provide their own cover art and jacket design? If so, is it good, effective cover art?

Especially in digital publishing, your tiny thumbnail image of a cover has between *one tenth of a second to five seconds* to catch a reader's eye online. That's it. In that time, the reader has to be able to gauge the genre, the mood of the book, something about the content, the title, and the author's name. In that order, to be brutally frank.

For self-published authors: unless you are a Big Name author with a lot of fans, keep your author name smaller than your title.

If the author is offered or told to accept substandard art and font choices, does the publisher excuse it later by saying 'that's what the author wanted'?

Is the author a trained and competent cover designer?

Even then, authors with some cover design competency work *with* the publisher's art and marketing departments.

Can the publisher produce a professional product? Does their book look like a book? Part of the lamented 18 month-average from publishing contract to commercial publication involves revision, editing, and book design. Many badly-published small press, paid vanity, and self-published books reveal their rushed, unskilled origins with awkward formatting choices in ebooks or printed works.

Readers may not be able to identify the flaws, but they'll know something is wrong. Many of these 'tells' are just conventions left over from centuries of paper-and-ink printing methods. But they linger in the audience's mind as vague categories of *What a book should look like*. Ignore those conventions at your peril, especially in printed works.

Really bad covers and interior design are usually either a red flag for a publisher who doesn't care about selling books (because it may already have vanity publishing fees from the author), or a publisher who doesn't know any better (the Dunning-Kruger Effect, anyone?)

Often, it signals a publisher aiming for inexperienced vanity victims. I've seen several variations where the publisher works preferentially with teen and pre-teen writers, and excuses their bad covers as 'what the kids came up with'. Are the kids competent cover designers? Kid art can be cute and inspiring, but it's not always the best choice for a book cover.

Either way, an honest, skilled publisher would make sure author-provided cover art is of professional caliber, or use the author's concept to develop the actual cover.

A competent agent should not allow their authors to submit, insist upon, or accept substandard cover art. If you have an agent, and the agent lets one of your books go out with a truly horrible, unprofessional cover...take a good hard look at your agent.

And your artist! Cover art and design demands certain format choices that have become so customary they are ingrained into readers' sunconscious expectations of books. We can break those rules, but we have to do it effectively. If you are working with an artist new to cover design, make sure they know those rules.

Recent bad or awkward examples of cover art I've seen:

Numerous digitally-generated human figures used without post-rendering filters or brushwork to reduce the generating program's telltale smooth 'plastic' look. It really doesn't matter if the publisher/

game company claims, "Our audience doesn't seem to mind!" Your audience either doesn't know better (Dunning-Kruger, again) or overlooks it. Be certain that other people in your industry will not, while pointing and laughing.

Digital artifacts clearly showing multiple digitally manipulated image collages, often with mismatched proportions and light sources. (From several small presses and one big commercial imprint whose art department should have known better.)

Otherwise lovely Steampunk or Fantasy elements crammed so tightly into the cover that reading title and author in the thumbnail was very difficult.

Script fonts badly used in titles, especially with visually 'busy' backgrounds under the letters. Really, folks...is it too much trouble to see if your title font choice can be read or even seen, at thumbnail size?

Covers are big business and a driver of many sales. If your publisher isn't committed to providing the best cover possible given time and budget concerns, how well will they perform at other marketing tasks?

This goes for self-published authors, too.

I'm guilty in that some of my self-pub covers are better than others. I don't have the money right now to invest in too much professional cover art and design (not for my small sales). But I know the basics: it has to grab the eye at thumbnail size, the title has to be legible, there has to be enough neutral space for the title and author name, and the art has to be at least slightly interesting.

Nepotism Alert!

D oes the publisher appear to give preferential treatment to substandard works if they are from friends and family?

That's bad news any way you look at it: they're not professional, they don't have the necessary emotional distance to fairly assess manuscripts, and they may be treating their 'business' like a private ego-boosting club.

Every publisher will have authors it likes and favors: the highly visible, high-earning superstars. There's no way to get around that. One of the great conspiracy theories of self-publishing and vanity publishing insists that 'unknown authors never get promoted by the Big Five.' Which is wrong, and obviously so to anyone who has ever read Publishers Weekly, Locus, or any other professional publishing industry magazine.

While not every commercially-published book gets star treatment, it would be foolish of a publisher to avoid investing decent promo for all of its books. A lot of very effective marketing and promo by big and intermediate publishers completely bypasses ordinary readers, which is why authors sometimes believe the publisher is doing nothing.

Publishers try to pick books that will stand a chance of earning back their investment money and make a profit. That means the quality of all manuscripts should come first in the vetting process, no matter what relationship the author has to the publisher. If you hear rumors of such nepotism, try your best to verify them, but keep your distance until you do.

IS THE PUBLISHER OR agency allowing terrible behavior from junior members who might also be family, or preferred friends?

One of the worst cases of publisher nepotism I ever saw featured a literary agency with one of the junior members lying to authors, gaslighting authors, pitting clients against clients, lying to publishers, not bothering to submit manuscripts to publishers, refusing to provide that submission list to authors who asked, making serious profit off workshop fees to clueless new authors who wanted a 'superstar' agent, and vowing legal threats against any detractors. Faced with open proof of all of this, the agency...did nothing.

In another case, an agent who made a fairly big splash as a genre advocate was quietly moved from two separate agencies, one after the other, rather than outright being fired for lying to authors, raging at authors who asked for submissions lists, and attempting to blacklist authors who called out the agent. The agent is still in business at a third agency.

How can you be sure of anything in the agent-publisher querying game?

Sadly, you can't. So much about this industry takes place behind closed doors, outside the reach of social media. But a well-informed writer can even the odds by extensively searching online for problems with said agency or publisher. Follow Twitter, Facebook, and other social media sites. Pay attention to current events and rumors.

With libel laws being what they are in the United States, most of us can't outright say 'Agent So-and-so is a complete fraud' or "Publisher X cheats its authors'.

It's up to you to read between the lines.

Exclusives

Does the agent ask for exclusive consideration of a manuscript? Make sure it's for a specific period of time, not indefinitely. A couple of months is the longest acceptable time period for 'exclusive' consideration. Agents can effectively judge their chances with a manuscript in a few weeks, at most. They don't need six months to a year.

I understand the thrill an author gets when an agent or publisher says 'Yes' or even 'Maybe'.

Step back, breathe, calm down, and be clear-eyed and professional about what happens next. Do not let that *yes* or *maybe* blind you to some very bad behavior from the offering agency or publisher!

Does the agent state or imply their offers are so good that *authors should accept them without question*? Make sure the agent is worth that hype, first.

Few are...and the ones who are, generally don't behave that badly.

A manuscript good enough to get attention from one agent is probably good enough to snag a few others.

I heard about another new publisher whose owner actually called out an author for daring to *take a week* before responding to a contract offer. Most reputable publishers give at least two weeks, maybe more, depending on author accessibility. As expected, that publisher has shown itself to be something of a dumpster fire in other areas, too. I won't bother to mention them by name, because they flamed themselves out of business a few years ago.

The agent who originally inspired this chapter recently flounced out of the industry, presumably to go back to writing literary fiction. I feel bad for their authors, but I have to wonder how many they actually placed with a reputable publisher: the agent had little relevant experience and few industry contacts to begin with.

Looking through my list of science-fiction, fantasy, and romance literary agents (compiled from 2010 to 2019) I'd say at least ten percent of them have left the industry for reasons other than retirement or death.

Be careful when researching agents and publishers who demand exclusives from new authors. Is their time worth your time?

Do We Click?

Is this agent or publisher right for you?

So what if they have five mega-bestsellers listed this week in Publishers Weekly? Can they effectively represent or publish all of the genres you write, or think you might want to write? Everyone is different, and has different comfort levels. Research, research, research...and if you are unsure, ask them directly. It's more professional than backpedaling later.

If you are understandably cautious about approaching agents directly, observe them on social media. Hints about and reasons for an agent's extremely long response time, no response time, or leaving the business can often be seen in social media posts well before the problems become public.

Become familiar with an agent's client list and check back with it over time. When you see authors dropping off that list, check around places like WriterBeware, AbsoluteWrite, QueryTracker, and even the authors' social media feeds, to see if they are actively looking for or have found other representation. Then ask them if they can tell you why they left the first agent. Often, they can't, or don't want to. But you might get an honest, useful answer about whether to query that agent or not.

As with vanity publishers, it may be risky to rely only upon recently-signed authors for agent testimonials: they're still in the honeymoon period.

Same goes for small-press publishers: look around and see what their principal members are saying online. It might be eye-opening, and save you a messy severance later.

Politics matters.

Once upon a time, authors were willing to 'look the other way' if it meant getting a publisher or agent who could market them effectively. Most authors didn't care about politics, or if they did, were able to separate their politics from business.

That's no longer possible. Your agent and publisher should at least be on the same track as your core moral and ethical values. Otherwise, both parties might be wasting their time.

Publishers and literary agencies can change focus and collective worldviews, over time. It's worth it to do current research and see who 'fits', before you query them!

In the same vein, consider if there are there actual or potential conflicts of interest.

This can be a hard one to nail down, with the number of legitimate literary agencies who are opening boutique publishing arms (usually just digital, and usually just for existing clients' backlists.) Or the genuine publishers who see an unknown's mms that isn't quite *there* yet, and refer the author to legitimate, verifiable editing and writing-coaching services.

Reprint publishing can be a miracle for midlist authors and the readers trying to find their out-of-print books. Tanya Huff's wonderful *The Fire's Stone* was long out of print and getting hard to find on Amazon, when it was given new life by a literary agency's boutique imprint. There are a couple of invitation-only, independent cooperative presses who are rebuilding lost backlists. They are helping authors every day, and making readers like me drool.

But there is incredible potential for abuse if the agency/publisher isn't open about its process. What if the agency is accepting 'paying' authors for vanity publishing schemes, especially if those authors were rejected by the 'literary' side of the agency? Again, the agency/publisher is saying: "We don't want to pay you to publish your work, because we don't think it will sell well enough to be worth the effort...but we'll take your money and a cut of sales, to publish it for you."

Another trick is to 'refer' substandard authors to supposedly independent book doctors and other paid editing services. Sometimes these 'independents' offer kickbacks to the referring agency. Sometimes, as in the case of several notorious swindler agents, the book doctors, coaches, and independent press...you guessed it...are all sockpuppets of the founding agents and/family members. Sometimes unscrupulous agents can get kickbacks or perks from vanity publishers, for steering paying clients their way.

Sometimes the agent means well, but there isn't enough separation from the literary agency side and the for-profit editorial services side. (There's one particular well-known agency that does this, and keeps spinning off new agents and new boutique publishers who appear to think this is standard business. It can be a hot mess for authors, so look out.)

Dig deep. Do your own research. Decide what level of separation you can handle, and what the agency/publisher history reveals about its reputation. If an agent or a publisher didn't think enough of your work to say 'yes' from the start, what are they really getting by recommending you to someone else?

No means 'No', no matter how it's dressed up.

Also, just because you've been talking to a Big Five (Big Four, by now?) imprint, one of the gigantic multi-headed commercial publishers...doesn't mean you are safe. Many of them still have their hands in the unsavory vanity publishing world, via 'imprints' run by one or two of the most horrible vanity publishers around. So far, I have not seen actual proof of commercially-rejected authors being steered toward such vanity operations. But be aware the main publisher can get direct and indirect financial benefit from the victimization of vanity-published authors, through the legal filter of the vanity subcontractor.

Contracts

Does this agency or publisher have questionable contract terms? The agency should very clearly spell out how and when it pays out the author's share of royalties. What expenses the author will be charged for, and how those will be paid. To what extents will the agency go to submit works to reputable publishers, and to offer those submission records to authors? How easy will it be to end the agent-author relationship?

Submission records are a big issue, when it comes to authors leaving agencies. Why? We authors have to know which publishers an agent picked to see our manuscripts, so we don't accidentally send the same work out to the same publisher who already said 'No'. Or worse yet, a 'Maybe'. That can create a situation where the author might end up owing royalty commissions to two separate agencies: the new one and the old one who initially submitted the manuscript, and could claim to be entitled to earnings from it.

Publishers, especially small, newer ones, can have very opaque contracts.

If pressed on their terms, does the publisher retreat into, 'Oh those silly legal terms, we only have those in there because our lawyers say we have to. We'd never in a million years enforce them.' Then tell the publisher to strike them out. Or just walk away, because if really abusive terms are written into the contract from day one, you'll be wondering what else the publisher will spring on you.

I watched an online discussion unfold about a small-press contract that effectively made the author pay $5000 USD to release rights, plus 'extra' money based on the book's previous performance and potential 'lost income'. Another clause seemed to demand the author give the same publisher everything they write, regardless of genre, until the end of time. (And this publisher had passionate defenders, too.)

This isn't as far out in left field as you might think. Ellora's Cave, a now defunct but once-respected erotic romance publisher, laid down stringent rights release terms in order to stem the hemorrhage of profitable authors from its catalog. While I won't name amounts, I have seen individual book buyout numbers that could have purchased a rather good car. Several other small romance publishers have buy-back terms for rights revisions.

I don't like the idea of holding rights hostage for any amount of money, and I believe contracts should be written with clear reversion thresholds that are fair to both author and publisher.

Even if the publisher is staffed by wonderful, skilled, and sympathetic people, authors need to sign contracts with the knowledge that at any moment their perfect publisher could be taken over by sociopaths with bottom-feeding lawyers on speed-dial. Protect yourself and learn how to read publishing contracts.

Publishing contracts can be very complex, but there are resources to help you understand and negotiate them. Here's a useful overview from the University of Utah, with links to the Nation Writer's Union. *https://campusguides.lib.utah.edu/publishingcontracts*

Who Found Whom?

Did you find them, or did they find you?

It matters.

From what I've seen in this industry, 'real' agents and publishers are usually too busy to troll for clients. If they contact you first, watch out! Be wary of offers you didn't initiate through queries, twitter-pitches, convention meetings, referrals, or other actions on your part. Even then, be wary: previous chapters have pointed out agencies and publishers who essentially troll conventions and workshops, looking for unsavvy authors to milk for money in exchange for dubious or ineffective 'services'.

Everyone wants to be wanted. Everyone wants to be The Next Discovery, or at least be contacted out of the blue by a reputable publisher or agent who says: "We like what you are doing, and we want to help you do it."

The internet is wonderful. It makes breakout hits from unknown authors a little more possible these days. It publicizes the success stories.

The internet is terrible. Human psychology, legions of hopeful self-help books, and the accounts of successful self-published authors have convinced every writer they could be that very next superstar...with a little help. Agents and publishers who approach authors first, are often literally banking on the tendency of inexperienced, desperate authors to accept the first company approaching them.

Go on, be flattered by the attention.

Then be politely skeptical and do your research.

A legitimate agent or editor won't mind. A predatory or unprofessional one might rescind the offer and flounce off, often with threats of industry-wide blacklists and reprisals. (Don't believe that, either. They have no power over you or your writing career...until you give it to them, by giving them your book.)

A side note on literary grants winners:

There are a few high-profile literary grants that create 'buzz' around the winners, often leading to agents and other talent scouts contacting them to offer representation.

If you are one such winner and you are contacted by agents...be polite, be skeptical, and do your background research just as you would in any other situation. Especially if you've already queried these agents in the past on other manuscripts (or even the winning project!). Would they treat you and your work any better now, or are they just attempting to make bank on your newfound reward?

Crowdfunding Publishers

Does the publisher hint, infer, or outright suggest that its authors turn to crowdfunding ventures in order to pay 'their share' of publishing costs?

Most publishers underfunded enough that they can't make the investment in their books (and rely on the author to pick up all or 'part' of the tab) are essentially *vanity publishers*.

Or a small press publisher that may not have enough capital to survive its first few years of operation (which is why many more-seasoned writers say about small presses, "Wait a few years!")

Vanity publishers are unlikely to have the editorial skills or the marketing resources to sell many books. They've already been paid by the authors, so why should they?

That said, crowdfunding has a valid presence in publishing.

Reputable editors, authors, and groups are turning to crowdfunding more often these days to gain working capital. There's nothing wrong with it, as long as all parties are upfront and have a good reputation in the business (of knowing their business, and actually producing a real product).

Some crowdfunded projects run by professionals with actual publishing backgrounds, for projects that I find really interesting: *Tales of the Emerald Serpent. Unidentified Funny Objects. Real Women in Practical Armor. Girl Genius.*

Exercise your research skills, look up crowdfunded publishers, and pay close attention to the amounts of money raised by many of the completed campaigns. The authors are not generally chipping in financially. They've written the stories. The crowdfunding campaign is there to convince readers to buy in up front, and get certain perks in return: first printings, related merch and swag, artwork, etc.

I would contrast that with a specific example of the wrong way to do things, but I'm not that cruel. Let's call it a memoir/health-related novel, semi-fictionalized, by a person who signed on with a vanity publisher. The author had no backers for the estimated $2000 cost. I see this 'pay my vanity fees' stunt more often than I thought I would, but I suppose the beauty of Kickstarter is that it's open to nearly everyone...until they get shut down for violating the service's terms and conditions.

So now I *will* be cruel: Readers and supporters, when an author's Kickstarter campaign mentions a publisher, research the publisher before you pledge.

Please don't crowdfund vanity published projects.

By doing so, you validate their predatory business model. The resulting book, if there is one, will probably be badly produced and sink like a stone in the market ocean. You are likely just throwing good money and wishes at a deluded victim being preyed upon by a heartless predator. Maybe without your help, the victim will go into debt in another way to fund their book. Maybe they'll wise up and find a better publisher willing to pay them.

Writers, don't work with publishers who push you to crowdfund your works...unless you and they know you can get the backing to do it the right way.

Display Sites

These large or small online platforms promise to be a community where writers can showcase their own work, beta-test manuscripts, build followers and writing groups.

Often, any stories 'published' this way are behind a passworded digital wall, which can help the writer protect work from plagiarism and keep their publishing 'first rights'. Themed contests can bring writers more attention from readers, small presses, and major publishing companies.

Note: the commercial publishing industry has conflicting views on display sites. Some hold that works exhibited on such sites have, in fact, been published, and cannot be contracted for the more lucrative 'first rights'. The publisher might ask if the writer has any unpublished fiction.

Other publishers have sought out writers whose work was first shown on display sites, and republished it without prejudice as long as the display site piece was taken down (often, also rewritten).

The problems with display sites can include: unskilled readerships perpetuating bad writing habits, the same fractures and pressures that influence smaller writers' groups, the sites' founders using the member base as a captive audience for clickbait advertising, and promising a better user experience with overpriced but often worthless 'deluxe' memberships.

Display sites are often a fun and riotous community building deep social ties. To a reasonable extent, you'll often be rewarded by higher participation.

But don't expect a multimillion-dollar commercial publishing contract out of it!

Convention Hucksters

D oes the publisher or literary agent spend a lot of time at literary, media, and/or writer's conferences?

While at such functions do they aggressively build and use their contact lists to market author-paid workshops, classes, cruises, residencies or other services?

Does the agent appear to excessively tout their 'Number 1' status in a genre, or in an industry publication's poll numbers? Beware: that status might not mean what you think it means!

Respected, effective agents usually don't advertise this way. They don't need to. The ones who do market themselves like this usually have another angle, often courting convention and workshop appearance fees or their own marketing hype.

Hype works because it attracts the attention of new, hopeful writers, some with a stunning manuscript. Shady agent uses hype to get eyeballs, and thus vacuums up lucrative projects that might have gone to other agents.

Case in point, with no names mentioned: a major agent with a big firm has recently been alleged to have taken on authors they never intended to seriously represent, all to further the agent's claim as being a 'number 1 agent by volume of sales'. Note here that volume doesn't necessarily mean *quality* of sales. The agent is also alleged to have misrepresented publishing deals to both authors and the publications, in some cases completely rewriting fraudulent contracts to make deals look better to authors than they actually were.

The sad truth is that this agent has been a career-builder for many of their star clients, and they are unlikely to get punished at this agency. I can't even tell you who it is.

Agents like this might be making as much or more money from workshop fees, than from selling books to publishers.

The average writers conference (pre-Covid) was a hothouse of authors paying for face time with agents and editors. While 'digital' conventions made the most of Covid-era distancing, in-person conventions will come back.

Convention-going authors are a captive, willing audience predisposed to think favorably on any professional conduit to success. I've looked at the membership lists and event schedules of many writers' conventions, and time after time seen listed agents and publishers I'd consider problematic business partners. As with twitter pitches in publishing, research your options before you pay or sign up for pitch time with a convention-going agent or publisher.

A new-ish thing linked to the popularity of Twitter-pitch contests and other social media pitch support groups: winning a 'free' entry to an agent-or-publisher-workshop/conference. Be careful. If you're not local, you'll be out travel, hotel, and food expenses at the very least. You may or may not get solid, valuable information at these events, and network with reputable literary agents, editors, and media influencers. Some offer more value than others. Some exist to pitch the agency's side businesses and partners, as thinly disguised Multi-Level-Marketing pitches with a literary slant. As with any professional conference, research the presenters and participants before you enter the contest or accept the 'win'.

Are these credible within their industry? Would you want to work with them?

Diversity

Is diversity in author/character race, creed, sexuality, etc. important to the agent or publisher?

How do they define 'diversity'?

Does their definition actually foster diversity?

How will they support diverse authors?

And how are they going to monetize diversity for their gain and the diverse author's loss?

Yes, that last one is cynical, but just look at the recent social media outcry over #ownvoices being hijacked against the intentions of the hashtag's originators.

As with religious publishers, know about the potential bias issues before you query or submit work. Does the publisher or agent show a demonstrated track record of supporting diverse books? Or is this a feel-good slogan smokescreen they use on Twitter and other social media? You might be able to learn more by looking at their back catalogs, QueryTracker, and Publisher's Marketplace entries.

The same goes for writers' organizations.

The Romance Writers of America imploded in late 2019 and early 2020 over its lack of diversity and its horrible treatment of romance writers from often-marginalized groups. It seems to be rebuilding now under more-diverse and mindful guidance, but many romance writers are taking a 'wait and see' approach to returning to national or local RWA chapters.

There's a magazine I will never submit another story to, because a few years back it hosted a spectacularly bad gaffe of White Privilege. That story infuriated me, and the editors' double-down reactions didn't help.

2015 and 2016 seemed to be great years for POC, OwnVoices, and LGBTQ authors to finally get some platform help (the US Presidential election aside). There is still a lively debate sloshing around social media about who is and is not eligible to benefit from these efforts.

One of the reasons why I worry about this debate is its tendency to further splinter groups which should very well be allies.

Just look up 'Biphobia in Publishing'.

I mostly have a problem with publishing industry professionals who at least appear to be paying lip service to the Issue of the Month, with no intention of actually doing anything about seeking and representing marginalized voices.

Or agents, editors, and reviewers who insist that a marginalized writer writing about marginalized characters and cultures is ONLY valid as long as they stick with (white mainstream expectations) of those cultural expressions.

Or if the diverse author is expected to wallow in emotional pain and issue-driven drama, instead of simply telling their story...whatever that may be.

This behavior is dangerous to all diversity-valuing writers in the era of authoritarian governments, amped-up Culture Wars, and tribal Balkanization. We need to stand together in the face of implacable opposition, not shatter into ineffective social clubs.

A side note on Sensitivity Readers and the #ownvoices movement: we need this. If you are writing in (especially a historical or contemporary) culture not your own, please run it by (and PAY for) someone qualified to tell you when you're being clueless. If you are a writer from a non-mainstream background, we need your words now more than ever.

But don't confuse your Sensitivity Reader for a priest granting you complete and eternal absolution, or use them as an excuse for continuing to be clueless.

Are They Bullies?

Does the publisher/agent/marketer/editor use fraudulent DMCA take-down notices to strong-arm its critics into removing negative information like bad reviews or allegations of bad behavior?

Do they regularly use real DMCA notices to remove anything they deem 'their property', as in quotes from their books and their website copy used by detractors to call out bad business practices? Do these companies overuse take-down notices, but are legally within their rights to do so?

In any case, this can be a hint you are dealing with a very hair-triggered and ultra-sensitive organization, and you might want to step back before they drag you into their business and their online wars.

There are churches and political groups that use this tactic as one of their main offenses against critics...so go on the alert instantly when you see this *from any company*. They could turn on you, too. At the very least, if you are a blogger or reviewer using Fair-Use quotes in your work, educate yourself about what to do if you think you've been targeted by an erroneous or fraudulent take-down notice.

The Digital Millenium Copyright Act was one of the most ill considered pieces of legislation in the unwieldy American copyright system, and has been one of the most abused. It's hard for genuinely-infringed creators to use against piracy. It's easy to twist for fraud and extortion, in my limited opinion.

I won't name it here, but the specific company that inspired this section has its own page on www.absolutewrite.com. The company *used an allegedly fake DMCA copyright notice about a review blog it didn't own and has no control over*, to force a third party (AW) to remove flagged content.

It didn't work.

Another red flag, which I've mentioned before but should bring up again: does this company or individual use NDA (non disclosure agreements) and/or SLAPP (lawsuits intended to censor, intimidate, and silence critics with the cost of a legal defense, to make them abandon their criticism or opposition)?

If they've done any of that once, they'll probably do it again.

Do you really want to do business with such a company? You could either become one of their targets or accomplices.

Agent/Writer Alert

This one is more about literary agents, than editors or other publishing professionals.

Does the agent also write their own novels and non-fiction? In your target genre? Are they a newish agent? If all those points apply, you may want to be cautious in querying or working with them.

They may not stay in the agent game much longer.

Being a new literary agent can be hard, low-paying work. Agents generally do this because they love books and stories. It takes time to build enough of a client list to generate living wages for the agent!

When a still-new agent gets a book deal of their own, that may take up more and more of their time, leaving you out in the cold. Check the agent's social media feeds to find out how invested they are in their agent work, how happy they are about their own publishing, and how much of their time gets split between those.

I know of some older, experienced agents who are very successful at balancing the job of writer and literary agent. They've had time to invest in their agenting career, to build a large stable of hopefully competent writers. They have industry connections, so when it comes time to market their own fiction and nonfiction, they're probably not competing directly with slush-pile entries. They're most likely going to be professional about it.

Junior agents who've just gotten in the agent game already operate under deep risks. Adding their own writing career may be too much of a workload for them to handle, and very rarely are they going to give up on their potential writing career. Would you, in the same situation?

Add to the fact that if they are writing in your genre, with possibly similar markets, themes, etc...now they are your direct competition. How much can you trust the agent's objectivity between pitching/promoting their work and yours?

I only mention this point because since I've been querying works (starting in 2009), I've watched a number of younger agents abruptly abandon agenting for other careers.

New agents burst onto the scene with enthusiasm and determination, pulling along happy clients by force of will. And a few years later I've seen those same agents get a decent book deal of their own, drift away or drop clients, and in some cases leave agenting completely.

Some handled their departure with grace, handing off clients to replacement or recommended agents.

Some lost interest in submitted works, in some cases 'losing' manuscript submissions when acquiring editors left a publisher and didn't notify the agent.

Some neglected necessary or publisher-requested editing and revisions.

Some just vanished.

In the worst cases, the agency failed as well, by not helping the clients find new agents in-house or outside...and then threatening the clients when they want to go public with the problems.

It's worth repeating as often as you can stand to read it: *Being published badly is worse than not being published at all.*

Being represented by a bad or indifferent agent is worse than not having an agent at all.

To go along with this topic: is the agent's website and other social media swamped with content about his or her own writing or other side hustles? Is it handled well, or clumsily? You could be looking at someone more interested in representing and promoting themselves, than other authors. In very bad scenarios, their awful online behavior won't look good if it's connected to you.

Let's Talk About Poetry

Specifically, about getting *paid* for your poetry. Use your Research-Fu to look up Poetry Writers markets online, and have a healthy bucket of skepticism ready.

In general, if you already have some fame or celebrity, or are at least known for your poetry, you might be able to get a big, reputable publisher to publish a chapbook of your work.

There are smaller but still laudable publishers who take on poetry chapbooks (single-author collections), for royalty publication, with similar limited earnings ($1500 to $5000 at best) as small-press novel-length prose works.

Some national and international charitable foundations have reputable poetry-related contests or grants opportunities, sometimes topping out at the $25,000 USD or more range.

Some magazines pay for poems.

However, any new small-press (that isn't a university press) accepting lots of different genres and *also* claiming to publish whole chapbooks of single-author poems...is probably a dead end.

Be especially wary of the vanity press versions of poetry publishers, who have honed their bait-and-switch on naive poets for nearly a century.

The game goes this way: they advertise that poets can win money and fame in the publisher's contests. They'll take almost anything that looks remotely like a poem. Nearly all entrants will 'win' inclusion in an hardbound 'library reference' book. The catch is that the happy author must pay steep prices to actually get a copy of that book. These contests are worthless as publishing credits, and exist only to get authors to buy hardback books.

I write and sell poetry...but I do it in the form of book art sculptures, where I can get paid at least a couple hundred dollars per poem.

Circling the Drain

Is the publisher claiming they are closing?

Then not closing, then offering waffling words about what they're actually doing? While still urging authors to send queries? While asking for huge fees for rights reversions?

Huge warning sign, meriting a lot more research!

Between 2016 and 2021 I've seen several publishers and platforms do this. It leaves authors and agents confused and angry. Stability is good for business. If I don't think a publisher is stable, I won't query them...and I might not even buy their books.

Other ways to judge stability:

Is the publisher bleeding authors? Pay attention to the publisher's author list. How many new authors do they sign every quarter? How many authors leave to either self-publish or go to another publisher? Of the departing writers, were they low or high sellers? If they went to another press, what is its reputation?

Authors and publishers shuffle around a lot, so this may or may not mean the first publisher has problems. But many recent publisher meltdowns have been heralded by waves of earlier author departures.

Entry Fees

If you are entering a literary contest with entry fees, be careful to research the contest to see if it has any publishing industry standing, a useful prize or prizes, and a fair judging system by experts in the genre...or at least a decently large sample of the voting readership.

Many such 'contests' are glossed-up money grabs trading a meaningless physical or digital 'award badge' for your entry fees. They may not be considered worthwhile by the bigger publishers and review sites in their genre. In some cases, these contests are run by industry groups that are little more than mutual admiration clubs for small-press publishers and even vanity publishers.

Instead of offering cash or a useful software prize, the winners often get 'free' or 'discounted' marketing packages, publication offers, and other services that may end up costing more money, and offer little positive visibility if they are not attached to quality representation or publication.

They probably won't get the contest-winning authors blacklisted by big publishers (that rarely happens in publishing, but usually only when the author is an utterly difficult person to work with.)

I have seen *anecdotal* hints that some pay-contest authors, agented or not, may face pushback when they do aim toward bigger publishers: less favorable contract terms, shorter contracts, and possibly fewer new contracts. I haven't seen any direct correlation of this, however, and it would be worth deeper study.

Often the paid-contest judging consists of a popularity contest by a relatively few number of readers or participants on online comment forums. You can spot this when authors splash 'vote for me!' notices across social media.

Why do this? Because some authors are naive, and happily give their money away. Some are cynical, and have learned that in some genres their readers can be attracted by any signal of quality, however real or spurious. These authors understand that a $30 to $50 entry fee is cheap advertising to get a few dozen more book sales or mailing list subscriptions, whether or not the actual contest is 'real'.

How to guard against it? Research. How old and established is the contest? Is it sponsored or endorsed by major publishers within your genre? Does it stick to one or a few literary genres/styles/cultures...or does it try for dozens of different categories? As with vanity and over-extended small presses, a large number of genres may indicate a lack of focus or expertise.

What is the ulterior motive? And who is behind the contest?

This matters.

Large religious organizations and foreign governments have been alleged to use literary and art contests as image rehabilation for their own dubious activities, even if the recruited authors or artists are not affiliated with those faiths or countries.

Weird Practices and Trigger Fingers

Does the publisher insist that all of their authors remove all references to trademarked, copyrighted, and/or branded items, models, places, etc?

Use only generic terms or made-up place names?

There's one very small romance press that apparently ran into trouble once, when a trademark holder objected to having their property mentioned in a novel. Hence, this draconian protective reaction. Personally, I think that's a bit insane in the other direction, and the press in question doesn't show strong enough sales to justify the restriction. But they have authors willing to abide by their rules, so who knows?

Legal threats are a definite chill factor in modern business.

To a lesser extent, many small presses have contracts which absolve them of any legal obligation if the writer gets sued by an outside party. Some contracts will hold the author liable for even the publisher's legal fees, if the latter gets dragged into the mess.

Read your contracts, gauge your comfort level with potential liability, and know what's actually in the contract language.

I can say from watching other people's misadventures that The Walt Disney Company (tm), anything related to Dungeons & Dragons (tm), and the Terry Pratchett (tm) estate are absolutely not groups authors want to tangle with. These entities are known to mount a quick and muscular defense of property terms and images. This isn't necessarily a bad thing (although I have strong feelings about Disney's obvious and hypocritical misuse of copyright in many cases).

Do You Wanna Be Right or Rich?

More politically incorrect stuff! It's never been easier to self-publish, and the rewards can be vast for some lucky and/or well-placed authors.

But as with any burgeoning industry, there's often more cash to be made in fleecing investors.

I know of several 'self-pub writers support groups' who are essentially cults-in-the-making, and share a lot of cult tendencies. They push the following methods to become 'best-selling' authors: writing to popular trends, writing quickly (sometimes one or two books a month), exhaustive research in bestselling keywords, covers, tropes, etc. Their fiction and non-fiction can verge from sublimely well-done to ridiculously bad.

They'll often share conspiratorial, militaristic, apocalyptic, anti-science, fringe-right OR far-fringe left beliefs in their fiction and outside it.

Money matters more than message, though, with many of these writers. If not writing self-published 'bestsellers' (usually momentary bestsellers created by manipulating sales and Amazon categories), these authors might be involved in multi-level marketing, risky stock market trades, bitcoin hustles, house-flipping, and illegal arms sales (Or do all of those simultaneously. I wish I was kidding, but I'm not.)

I recently witnessed a self-proclaimed 'good Christian' writer tell a less-wealthy and experienced author protégé: "Do you wanna be right or rich?"

And they're not the only person glorifying wealth above all else, in those types of writing clubs. Be aware that these writers' groups and their associated publishers can form extreme cliques, ready to manipulate 'lesser' authors for the advantage of 'favored' authors, and savage those who seem to stray from the dominant groupthink.

If new writers are comfortable with that hypocritical worldview, so be it. I decided a few years ago I'd rather be comfortably-paid, enjoy my writing, and be able to sleep at night...so I got a job in manufacturing.

Writers' Magazines

D on't get me wrong: I like *Writer's Digest*, *Publishers Weekly*, and many of the other paid periodicals and free forums aimed at writers. They often have useful tips, industry news, and inspiring interviews. Publishing industry periodicals give those of us outside the environment an invaluable glimpse into the industry. When I read them I don't feel quite as alone in my writing life.

However, there's a dark side to most of these periodicals, which newer writers often don't learn about until it's too late:

The advertisers found in such publications.

Magazines need advertisers to help defray the cost of production and distribution. A periodical aimed at writers is logically going to host advertisers trying to reach those writers. Such services can include commercial and vanity publishers, editors, literary agents, cover designers, self-publishing services, special interest industry group memberships, book packagers, writers' guilds and groups, writing contests, and workshops and retreats.

Reputable and responsible publishers, editors, literary agents, and other publishing professionals do hang out their shingle and advertise in writers' magazines and online forums.

But they usually have enough work from existing clients, client recommendations, and prospective clients who know how to professionally network and research.

Meanwhile, new and relatively unskilled 'professionals' may use such periodicals to find new clients who may be just as ignorant about the market.

Predatory agents and publishers, bogus workshop operators, and fake contest scammers often seem to make up a large proportion of other advertising space, and may even be listed in more-professional columnists' interviews and profiles, or as members of otherwise legitimate industry groups. It's not necessarily because the publication/group is run by 'evil' people. Just busy ones, who may not have time to do anything but take an advertiser's credentials (and cash) on faith.

So it's safer to apply 'Trust, but Verify' to any advertiser in a writers' magazine, whether print or digital. (The same goes for books promoted by local interest or regional magazines and newspapers, but that is another chapter.)

Even the biggest commercial publishers have vanity-publishing arms or associates.

These pay-to-play vanity publishers invest large sums in online and print advertising with writers' magazines. They appear at local and regional book fairs with professional-looking booths and presenting 'authors'. They regularly attempt to smear their detractors as 'unsuccessful authors' or former clients 'with a grudge'.

What can a new author do?

Take no appearance of authority for granted. Not mine (I'm just a part-time writer.)

Just because you see an advertisment on TV, the internet, or in a writers' magazine, do not assume that advertiser is automatically legitimate. You're safer to assume the opposite until you do diligent research that proves otherwise.

How do you research? Learn effective keywords, don't trust the first entries that pop up in your searches, and use your scam-detecting skills to figure out what that company is really about.

A publisher or agency using social media ads to solicit your novel probably isn't anyone you want to write for.

At least, not until you know a lot more about that company!

Academic & Scientific Paper Scams

The predatory vanity publishing world is not limited to fiction. Academic and scientific papers are also a hot commodity, since the legitimate markets can have high entry barriers in fees and vetting. A host of predatory and often outright criminal publishers have surfaced to 'serve' those customers.

Many scientists and academics need to publish work to promote their career, grants applications, or general reputation.

Many dubious presenters need an official-looking publishing credit to bolster their claims or products (similar to how vanity publishers use fake or problematic contests and associations to push their services.)

How to tell the difference, when many respected logical thinkers may not be able to?

Look for the same flops in logic you'd find in other anti-intellectual communities. The same meaningless jingoism, the same vague promises...and often, the same exorbitant publishing fees!

The US and Europe have their share of these outfits. But a large number of them are based in India, Southeast Asia, and Africa. All of these regions combine rising markets, powerful legitimate publishers, brilliant academics, knowledge-hungry students, large amounts of money, predatory vanity publishers, and viciously divisive nationalist politics.

Here's a link to Scholarly Open Access. *https://scholarlyoa.com/*

And Beall's List of predatory and fake journals. *https://scholarlyoa.com/publishers/*

If you find a 'journal' listed here, it's worth taking your time to be skeptical before you decide to submit to it!

Here's a link to Brian Dunning's 'Skeptoid' podcast about fake academic publishers and the white hat hoaxers who help expose them. *https://skeptoid.com/episodes/4543*

Just for laughs...and the learning experience!...here's a Wiki link to the time when SF writer Isaac Asimov thoroughly trolled a scientific journal that wasn't paying attention. *https://en.wikipedia.org/wiki/Thiotimoline*

Here's John H. McCool in The Scientist 'Opinion: Why I Published in a Predatory Journal'. *https://www.the-scientist.com/critic-at-large/opinion-why-i-published-in-a-predatory-journal-31697*

Why is this a worldwide problem? Who does it harm?

A lack of properly vetted and researched scientific and academic work hurts all countries' scientific intelligence quotient.

It allows for easier plundering of whole economies by special interests using 'fake news' to advance their agenda. It covers and excuses wars and genocides.

It promotes simplistic thinking and Orwellian Double-Speak over difficult but worthwhile truths.

It has specific individual human costs, as when cancer patients choose ineffective bogus treatments over proven science, based off poorly-researched work in fake journals. Or in the most recent worldwide example, when science-averse populations chose not believe warnings about the Covid19 pandemic...and chose again to avoid mask use and vaccinations.

It has cultural costs, too. When unprepared or corrupt professionals plagiarize other people's work or 'buy' their credentials, they're lying about their qualifications. It might slide by without anyone knowing, and no one may be substantially harmed by the deception. But it can also lead to career shame. Or now, when manifestly unqualified politicians in multiple nations have led to countless unnecessary deaths in wars, poverty, and disease.

Peer review, like democracy, only works when your peers are intelligent, critical-thinking, and well-read members of the wider community.

AgentFails

Not all literary agents are equal!
I should not have to say that.

It's a truth in current publishing markets, that an author in possession of a decent manuscript should at least try to find an a literary agent BEFORE approaching major publishers. I still stand by that, even though I wrote myself out of the agent-hunt for at least the near future.

Agents can open up and manage opportunities that most solitary authors don't have the time, training, resources, or contacts to do. That 15% the agents earn can mean thousands more dollars going to the writer, in the long run.

15% commissions can be easy money if a bad agent piles up enough of them.

In the last couple of years, I've watched the online fallout from several spectacular #AgentFails. I've mentioned some in other chapaters, but here is a quick rundown.

For legal reasons, I'm not going to name the guilty parties here.

One theme that crops up many times with these bad-agent horror stories is their sheer laziness.

They don't research to see which publishers & editors might be a good fit for a manuscript.

They take on far too many authors to give decent service to most of them, hope a few make serious money and justify support, and string along the rest.

They make a lot of outside income by offering workshops and online classes, some of which may or may not actually help writers hone their craft and successfully query an agent or publisher.

They tell their writers they're submitting work when they haven't, and can't or won't offer a submissions list when called out.

They submit to sub-par publishers in hopes of that 15%, or even worse: they get kickbacks from the publisher.

They're in colluding with 'editorial services' promising a publisher-worthy manuscript (at a high price to the author, some of which gets kicked back to the referring agent.)

They are extremely litigious and combative online, to the point that authors already in their 'stable' are afraid to rock the boat. Worse, those authors often recommend their agent to other authors, in hopes of Ponzi-scheming their way to better earnings.

If the agents advance in their field, they teach this bad behavior to newer agents. If they cut and run away from the industry, they can leave behind stranded authors.

AgentFail, the Fanfiction Edition

A case-study dealing with fanfiction, but applicable to other writers.

Fanfiction is one area where a few authors have broken out as high-earning commercially published original fiction writers, so some literary agents are interested in seeking out talented fan writers.

Fanfiction writers enjoy high visibility in the genre publishing world right now. Archive of Our Own's recent Hugo Award win (itself a source of much controversy, backpeddling, and industry confusion) means that great fanfiction writers are getting much more scrutiny from publishing industry scouts. Many fan writers are already seasoned professionals with multiple commercial writing credits; semi-anonymous fanfic is just where they go to play.

But there's a sizable proportion of fanfiction authors who are talented amateurs with no publishing experience. They're the ones most at risk from predatory literary agents and publishers, and the ones least trained to protect themselves.

I know of several cases where unagented fanfiction authors were approached by A Publisher asking about original manuscripts. The authors expressed interest in the publisher's offer, but asked for time to get an agent's representation.

The same agent, in each case.

These authors approached this agent, who basically said, 'Sure I'll represent you! Sign over your 15%!'

Then the publisher said, 'We took your expression of interest as a legal *Yes*, so now you're signed with us!"

Then the agent said, 'Because this publisher said this, it counts as prior arrangements. I cannot now negotiate any part of your contract. But I still get 15% of your eventual sales!'

This is seriously dirty pool. I can only hope the agent is actually doing right by some of their higher-earning authors, because if not, we're going to see court cases in the near future. I pity any agency where this agent lands, because they are exposing the entire agency to legal wrangling. This particular agent has a lot of other questionable practices, too, such as not submitting requested work to publishers, not supplying submissions lists when authors request them, and moving (rapidly) through several different agencies.

The downlow: If you are a fanfiction writer, you are assumed to be a valuable but probably industry-naive resource.

Be careful what you tell publishers if they come to you.

Be even more careful about who you get to represent you.

Another AgentFail related to fanfiction: a highly-skilled fan writer (with beloved stories on several fanfiction display sites) was approached by a respected literary agent. Not to publish the fan work, of course, but some similarly-amazing original fiction. The author said 'yes', even though the agent insisted on the unrelated fan work being removed from all display sites. The agent sold the original novel to a large commercial publisher's *digital-only imprint*. This meant the work would probably not be offered as a trade paperback.

The novel was published to fanfare and some good reviews, as a groundbreaking queer fantasy exploring some new territory in older tropes (I can't get more specific than that.)

The second novel was published, also digital-only. The publisher was taken aback that it featured mostly different characters, and involved a less-mainstream approach to queer topics.

The publisher did not renew the contract for the third novel.

The author got their rights back and self-published all of the original novels. I have no idea if they are still represented by that agent.

AgentFail, the Diva Edition

A nother case-study, another agent and author.
Literary agents are human: they have likes, dislikes, foibles, and triggers like anyone else. Sometimes an author is lucky and their quirks will mesh with the agent's. This is one of the major reasons to exhaustively research agents before you approach them.

Commercial publishing is a rough business. As reasonably well-informed authors, we know literary agents offer our best shot at decent sales with a trade publisher. Agents...good agents...do a lot to earn their 15%.

Note: I've had two literary agents between 1992 and 2016. Both are lovely people and skilled professionals, and they would never dream of treating authors the ways I have listed.

Bad agents can ruin a writer's career, sanity, and their joy in writing. I've watched dozens of agentfails over the last decade, as I researched publishers, agents, markets, trends, and my fellow authors. It's not always easy to spot bad agents ahead of time.

What is a 'bad agent'? For this section I'm only talking about commercially successful literary agents, with excellent documented sales and large client lists...who have, with certain authors, failed so horrifically that other authors might want to be careful about querying them.

Very much like the current focus on sexual harassment in work & politics, I can't actually name these agents without opening myself to legal jeopardy. Their awful treatment of some authors is an open secret, if you take the time to research. Writer Beware and www.absolutewrite.com offer a depth of information going back many years. Simply watch for authors announcing they are seeking new representation, and track back through their & their ex-agent's social media posts.

This segment follows one particular author and agent, with enough of the serial numbers filed off for me and the author to remain safe. (The agent could be inflicted with boils and bedbugs, for all I care.) Do I know who it is? Sure, because I have basic research skills and a good memory.

Author: three well-received SFF novels from a large publisher. Books compared favorably to a master of the subgenre.

Agent: really well known in SFF community, but has some previous problematic social media gaffes.

Author was typically over the moon upon initial signing of first mms & two proposals, but noticed quickly that agent didn't pay attention to the next two books' outlines.

Agent obviously wanted a massive bestseller/award winner, and pushed that outcome over the author's story preferences. Agent insisted in being the sole go-between for author and editor, not allowing independent contact between the other two parties.

Agent secretly tried to rewrite books without author's input or permission.

Called on that no-no, Agent then withheld useful criticism during edit processes, but began complaining about the writing in published versions. Agent was incommunicado for long stretches of time. Agent began gaslighting author about poor sales and promo. Agent appears to have torpedoed the final book proposal, leading to its refusal from the publisher.

Finally, after several years, the agent 'fired' the author, essentially telling the author they were a terrible writer, a useless person, with no usable ideas and poor skills. That no respectable publisher would work with the author after seeing their poor sales. This shattered the author for almost a month, before serious intervention and their own resilience prompted the realization: 'That agent is a horrible person and seriously unprofessional'.

The author could look back and and see early warning signs, enough to agonize over 'I should have left earlier'. But we're authors, and it's damn hard to give up on having an agent, especially one advertised as having industry clout.

I'd previously queried that agent a couple of times for different projects, got form rejections, learned some squicky things about the agent on social media, and never bothered with them again.

I honestly hope they leave the business. How they treated this author is not an isolated case, but part of a pattern with this agent and agency.

Offers and Assumptions

I have begged literary agents before: *please clarify your stance on negotiating publishing offers for querying authors.*

We authors need to know beforehand, if agents never do this and would rather we not contact them with outside publishing offers, or if it is something the agent might consider doing on a case by case basis.

If you are a literary agent, please put this in your guidelines, blog posts, Tumblr, whatever. We'll be grateful and not bother you.

Otherwise, things like this are going to happen, leaving agents furious, authors confused and angry, and publishers in limbo.

Let's talk about offers of publication, offers of representation, and the assumption of offers.

I have a writer friend who has a great mms. It's hard to pin down in genre, but it has good bones and a good editor will turn it into a dazzler. Friend has been trying to get this book in front of agents for a while, through queries, twitter pitch contests, etc. Friend finally gave up on those, and subbed directly to some interesting small-press publishers.

Some of which I liked and some I didn't, but it's not my book at stake. Friend got enthusiastic responses from three publishers, and was left with The Choice:

1. A newish press with very little to recommend it yet.

2. A stellar independent press with new capital investment and serious editorial and marketing power.

3. A quiet, niche-focused, but fairly professional press with apparently the same core passions as Friend, and some decent plans for the future.

Friend wrote all three and asked for time. They granted it. At the same time, Friend emailed one of the agents who had asked for a query letter during a recent Twitter-pitch event.

Agent agreed to look at mms.

It was then I started shaking my head and mouthing the words, 'Make no sudden moves and back away slowly' to Friend. Because I have seen some of the online and behind-the-scenes meltdowns Agent has allegedly caused or enabled, going back to the agency where Agent learned to do these things. But again, not my circus, not my monkeys.

Agent...made a tentative offer on just a chapter or so. This is not unheard of, but it's really strange for a new writer's first book. Most agents want the full manuscript, so they can see where the story goes, and if the author is actually able to produce a complete book.

Friend sent off mms, and reminded Agent there were offers on table. Friend asked for a value-added statement from Agent, as in 'What can you do for me that I can't, in these current markets?'

No further word from Agent. For over a month. Faced with offers and ticking clocks, Friend finally stepped back from agent-hunting and took offer #3 from the Nice Little Place. Sent a polite email to Agent, to thank for the time and consideration spent.

Only Agent had just cross-posted, apparently anticipating Friend's acceptance, and sent an editorial letter with suggested changes and some other markets. A few minutes later, Friend got a terse email generally concerned with the wasting of time, the bypassing of protocol, and unprofessional behavior.

Bear in mind, the Agent made no formal offer of rep, set no timetables, did not contact Friend at all after the first gushing comments on the first chapter read. There's even some worry on Friend's part that Agent was planning on collecting an easy 15% for 'negotiating' the already-issued offer from the Nice Little Place.

And then Agent tweeted about it in public, in terms both snide and histrionic.

I can actually see Agent's POV, and the assumption that Agent did a favor and was rebuffed. I know a few weeks to a month is probably not a good time limit on deciding whether to rep a book or not, let alone an author.

But this is WHY professionals trained by professionals FIRST make formal offers with specific timetables, expectations, and concessions...so nobody jumps the gun and writes what they think of as a 'wasted' editorial letter. Or assumes that they are the One, the Only, and the Perfect Choice.

Oh, and Nice Little Publisher? Turned out to be a hot mess.

HERE'S A CASE FROM my own query history.

I'd submitted a space opera novel query to ten literary agencies from late 2011 to early 2012, and either heard crickets, courteous 'not for us', or outright 'Ewwww, too queer' rejections from the agents involved. Then I queried five erotic romance small-press publishers. Two expressed interest. I queried one more literary agency I'd really liked, with the subject heading 'Publishing Offer'.

I'd hoped that this agency would take the small-press offer as a sign that maybe the book could do well with a large commercial genre publisher.

What happened instead was a terse reply that the agency would not even consider manuscripts with publishing offers they did not generate in-house from the start.

I went with one small-press publisher, and worked with another agent on the contract.

Now, looking back, I would have been better served to trunk the manuscript until the commercial market became more queer-friendly...or self-published from the start.

RISKY AUTHORS

This section is about our fellow authors. Get a sense of who they are before you engage with them in a writers' group, workshop setting, convention, critique partnership, or collaboration!

Drama Queens

H as an author published with a vanity publisher before? It's a strong indicator they will do so again with another vanity outfit.

Authors are an interesting club: we cheer each other on, enrich each other's lives, and occasionally descend into firestorm feuds with each other. We are our own agents' and publishers' best advertising ro other writers.

But sometimes, we are not to be completely trusted, even when we mean well.

An author you admire has just talked about their publisher, and offers to recommend you to them, or even just says: "You might try submitting work here."

Stop. Do a deeper social media dive on your friend.

Has this author published through a vanity publisher before? Multiple times? With different vanity publishers? If so, they've probably learned bad habits and/or misinformation about how publishing really works. They are very likely to pick yet another vanity publisher or substandard commercial publisher, shovel wads of money at them, and make the same mistakes again.

Follow them down that road at your own risk!

ON A RELATED TOPIC. how old is the author?

This is slated more toward authors seeking beta readers, critique partners, mentors, and writing buddies. It also works when evaluating writers' groups.

If the author is still in their teens, they may not really know what they want to do. They may have unrealistic ideas about a potential writing career, or be more focused on the trappings of fame than in doing the work behind the scenes. There's a fine line between admirable self-possession and willpower in the face of adversity—and utter cluelessness. A few leading questions can reveal whether time spent with very young authors may be worthwhile or wasted.

How do I know this? Because, duh, I was one of those late-teen clueless idiots. A lot of very kind people with a lot of experience tried their best to set me on saner paths. Sometimes they were successful. Often, not. I didn't make my first 'real sale' until I was 35, mostly because I was an idiot in an echo chamber.

If the authors are (often male, but I have seen this from female authors, too) retired or semi-retired, often between the ages of 55 and 75, and are just now starting to write-with-intent-to-publish, be wary!

These are the folks who can appear, along with the very young, to be the preferred targets of vanity publishers and less-scrupulous self-publishing gurus.

These are the folks who definitely are set in their worldviews, may have picked up some bad habits and information, and can be very resistant to different ideas. Six of the most bitter flamewars and authorial disasters I've witnessed over the last ten years have been started when age 55+ writers got called on their publishing industry misinformation, reactions to reviews, bad cover art, and/or publishing strategy.

I am NOT saying all young writers or all middle-aged writers are walking disaster areas. I know major science fiction and fantasy authors who published in their late teens, and have gone on to decades of success. I know writers who fired up the word processor after they retired, and became award-winners with dozens of books behind them.

But I've seen the reverse just often enough to include it as a data point, for deciding when I'm not engaging with a fellow author under anything but the most businesslike, controlled conditions.

Be especially wary of working with the Flouncing Professional, who seems to think that because they are a big deal with years of experience in one field, that they are a fabulous and stellar fiction author, too. Sometimes that skill translates. Sometimes not.

I've seen this behavior often from Silicon Valley techbros stampeding into publishing with Grand Ideas about how they want to 'shock and improve' the industry. Not every new idea will be Google or Amazon. It rarely works well for the techbros or the people following them, because publishing is a strange business.

Publishing is hard on the psyche until one develops a thick skin and a sense of perspective.

It's very tempting to glower at rejections, bask in one's previous achievements, and think: 'Agents and editors who don't recognize pure genius and artistry are obviously just know-nothing hacks...' Most of the time, that mindset can be counterproductive to an author. It takes away from honest humility in the face of creation.

At the very least, it can be a disadvantage when agents and editors go researching an author, and find such comments on social media. Between two similar great manuscripts from different new authors, an agent or editor is more likely to approach the author who seems like less of a general pain-in-the-ass.

Snark can be valuable, too. I adore many snarky authors, agents, actors, and bloggers...but most of them can back up the snark with genuine skill and wisdom.

WHEN LOOKING INTO A potential writers' group either online or meeting physically, try to evaluate the interactions between members, and look out for these potential 'energy vampires'. The nicknames I've given them come from multiple meetings with multiple groups over the decades.

The Queen Bee. Often has founded or taken over the group. This person uses the group as their personal sounding board, cheerleading squad, cult, and ninja character assassins. The Bee might be famous or a minor-league 'big fish in a little pond', and may or may not be a skilled writer. Membership in the Bee Club means bending with the cult's rules and customs, but it can come with some networking perks if the Bee is a 'Name' author who can actually help you. If not, there better be other reasons to spend your time and energy in this group.

The Lecher. Aligned with Hugh Hefner and Silicon Valley Techbros, this older person gathers a writing group primarily to select and groom younger sexual conquests, often under the guise of 'guru' leadership, New-Age 'personal growth' exercises, or 'networking'. Don't fall for them, and decide if this club will help or harm you.

Notebook, aka the Perpetual Researcher. This person attends meetings, convention panels, and writer's groups with physical or digital notebook in tow, and focuses primarily on the celebrities or perceived celebrities in the room. Notebook's endless quest is to interview each of these people, take notes, and try to find the Secret Key to Being Published. I watched one of these, for 15 years at Southwestern US science-fiction conventions, *ask the same questions of every panel guest.* I never knew if they wrote an actual book.

Concern Sister/Brother. Inveigles themselves in as your tour guide to the group, will try to become your best friend, unless or until they decide you're a better writer than they are. Then they will attack and try to poison the group against you. If you have shared any secrets with this person, they're not secrets anymore. Often a would-be Queen Bee.

The Ranter. Having exhausted too many other routes, groups, and opportunities, the Ranter is a writer who blames everyone and anything else for their self-designated failures. Most writers have been the Ranter at one point. The Ranter *rants all the time.*

The Cut-down Club. Functioning as a mini-team or the whole group, this squad is held together by envy and bickering. When one person hits a writing goal or triumph, the others try to inflate their own achievements in response.

The Nice White Lady. I didn't make her up; she and her sisterhood are at the heart of the Romance Writers of America's club-wide fragmentation in early 2020. The NWL is generally a middle-aged, wealthier Caucasian woman, often a romance or fantasy writer, prizing decorum and civility in public while sharing outright racist comments and actions when she thinks she's in safer company.

LibertyBelle. Can be any gender. Tends to write military thrillers or grimdark fantasy. Is almost always distinguished by liberatarian views, conservative politics, hysterically-overplayed patriotism, materialistic hypocrisy, and their 'I got mine, screw you attitude'. Pre-2016, I think it was possible to enjoy groups containing one or more Belles or NWL. Now I think it's just exhausting and counterproductive.

The Therapy Writer, who gets an expanded section from caution and sympathy. Think carefully about engaging with a writer who uses their prose primarily for self-therapy reasons. All writers work at the crucibles of emotion. Some elevate the therapy portion of the exercise as an excuse for sloppy writing, and then take criticism of their work to mean criticism of them and denial of their trauma.

Misery memoirs still have their place. But there are probably a million trunked or self-published ones, in contrast to the fewer numbers of commercially published similar books that reach a widespread audience. So again, unless you are a caregiver doing your job or a close family member, it might be safest to stay away from such authors.

Be aware that therapy writers, misery memoir writers, and senior-citizen 'family history' writers seem to make up the bulk of vanity publishing victims. If someone in your family or social circle is getting sucked into a pay-to-publish 'opportunity' for such work, you might want to intervene before the trauma becomes financial as well as emotional.

Beware Author Endorsements

Is the product or service endorsed by a major author?

Be skeptical. Don't take their word at face value. That Big-Name author may not know the full details of the company they just touted. They may have done it as a favor to a friend or colleague, or just been caught up in momentary enthusiasm.

Take that endorsement as just another data point in your research, and look a little closer.

I had to add this one because one of my favorite science fiction and fantasy authors once gave an online recommendation for an extremely disreputable display site well known for its attempts to spam fanfiction writers into joining 'writing contests' (which are really just held to puff up the site's hit count for advertising $$$.) I have to hope the author only saw 'science fiction and fantasy writing contest' and didn't look deeper.

Likewise, with literary agencies who have the same associations. The very same display site apparently courted and got the aid of a fairly well-known literary agent. Guess who I won't be querying, hmm?

I really wish I dared post a direct link to the aforementioned display site, because they are horrible spammers and appear to be outright liars. They have at least 35 chat bots stalking Twitter, Facebook, and multiple fanfiction writing sites daily. They appear to offer major publication and publicity deals, but as far as I can see, it's still appears mostly a content-stuffing operation to get more members and more advertising money from their affiliate links.

Be very skeptical of publishers and literary agents cold-contacting you with offers. Unless you've queried them, pitched to them at a conference, or been recommended to them...these days, it's more likely to be a scam of some sort.

Do research on your writing community, too!

If you are involved in an online, local community, or national writers' group, how picky are they about accepting advertisements from risky publishers or literary agents?

These support groups can be wonderful for writers at any stage of publication...but treat them with the same skepticism you'd reserve for writers' magazines. They may not filter their calls-for-submission that well, and they are likely to have many members who are affiliated with aforementioned publishers or agents (possibly in the honeymoon or desperate denial phases of the relationship.)

I won't generally participate in multi-author blog hops anymore until I've researched every single author in the chain. Too many entries from vanity publishers, awkward small presses, or badly self-published authors can tarnish the whole blog hop.

Cold? Heartless? Maybe. But this is a business decision based on many years in commercial trade shows, not just writing. There's a reason why big art shows are juried in the first place, and why publishers have slushpiles for all the unagented queries.

More about Twitter pitch contests and other online author-pitch events:

Just because an agent or editor signs on to judge one of these events, does not mean those judges are completely legit! Some contest judges (and even hosts) can be associated with problematic agencies or publishers who already have a bad or uncertain record in the industry.

They may be so new they have no track record. It's up to every pitching author to research contest judges and pitch requests before submitting material to the requesting parties.

Be aware there can be a personal and business cost to your diligence. There is at least a chance that you can be blocked or banned by these same communities...if your expressed skepticism rocks too many boats and offends too many influential spammers. If you get a lot of value from the group, it may be worthwhile to just look the other way when you see predatory or incompetent businesses advertising. Protect yourself, look out for your friends, and watch for sharks.

Authors Defending Bad Publishers

Writers, their publishers, and their big red flags:

Recently on an online writers' forum, a pulp writer I know offered some ideas on the following snarky-but-sadly-accurate list. It's distilled from his years of reading the typical ways authors defend their substandard, clueless, or frankly predatory publishers. Upon talking to veteran authors, editors, and agents, I realized we'd all seen these excuses. (Our usual responses in parentheses.)

1. *Communication with the publisher was prompt and courteous.* (Of course it was, they want your money and your book. Well, certainly your money.)

2. *Working with the editor and cover designer was a delight.* (Maybe, but do they know what they are doing? We'd take skilled curmudgeon over friendly incompetent, any day.)

3. *Of course I never expected actual sales—after all, I'm not Stephen King.* (Good publishers publish to make money. You should expect to see some sales, if the publisher is actually in that business, instead of merely grabbing vanity fees from authors. Non-vanity small presses also use this excuse, based on their habit of publishing lots of low-selling books. They might make a few dollars off a few hundred different books, but individual authors are making pennies.)

4. *Yes, promotion and marketing are up to me and I'm proud of it. That's simply how things happen these days, even with big publisher authors. Ask anyone.* (Yes. Please ask anyone who knows how publishing works. If you are not James Patterson, then you probably don't have decades of marketing experience and an advertising budget to match. By all means,

market yourself. Just be aware you probably are not going to see Patterson-level sales because of it.)

5. *A contract where you give up almost everything for almost nothing is actually pretty reasonable. Ask anyone.* (Again, ask people who work in real publishing. You should gain in proportion for what you give. If you are giving up nearly everything, that's essentially a work-for-hire contract, and it should pay very well. Like, $15,000 to $30,000 per book minimum, because that's the lower end of what good ghostwriters earn. Go on, we dare you: tell your publisher they can have their life-of-author all-rights grab if they give you twenty grand in an authenticated cashiers' check.)

6. *No, I am not the owner nor the owner's spouse. I am but a humble honest author defending a humble honest publisher.* (You're either still in the honeymoon phase where your publisher can do no wrong. Or you've begun to realize your trust was unfounded but you're too ashamed to backtrack, as in the Sunk Cost Fallacy. Or you're a heartless manipulative shill hoping to drag other authors in this mess in return for 'favors' from your publisher. We've seen all three from the same authors, depending on the stage of the publisher's rise and fall.)

7. *I see I've stumbled into a nest of bullies and ruffians and therefore must bid you adieu!* (You either know you're in the wrong and you don't want to defend yourself, or your shame is so great you can't face opposition telling you what you should have realized much earlier. When people point out you are wrong, that doesn't necessarily make them bullies. Ruffians, we'll give you.)

There: seven excuses authors make about dubious publishers. When you see these, especially multiples from the same author, there's a strong likelihood the publisher referred to is not someone you want to deal with. And maybe not the author, either.

Reading and Researching

This applies to any writer, any genre. I just use science fiction and fantasy in this section, because they're some of the fictional genres I know best.

Do you know your genre?

Maybe you don't need to know the old, obvious, prejudiced colonizer-type classics, but you should know your genre's current stars and respectable midlisters.

Otherwise, you might be reinventing the wheel. Which can be done, but honestly, the likelihood that a brand-new author will be the one to do it...is very low. Increase your odds by knowing what other people are doing *right now*.

On three separate online writing forums, I've recently been treated to the same unfortunate spectacle: writers (often very young ones, but not always) who know very little about classic or even current science fiction and fantasy, and who want to write in the genre.

They don't read it, or they may not read much at all.

They may come to SFF from movie tie-ins, fanfiction, or Dr Who (and about 75% of those seem to have only seen post-reboot Who from the last fifteen years).

They may come from anime and manga, with the mistaken idea that anime is only about crazy hair, superpowers, and explosions, and struggle to tell similarly vivid stories in text form. (When someone comes to me with a bad case of *Dragon Ball Z*, I usually prescribe

Cowboy BeBop or *Ghost in the Shell*. Or at least *Trigun*. Vash has Hair and a Backstory.)

This is like announcing that, although you are overweight and out of shape, you will be entering a triathlon next week. Are you likely to win, or even place? Nope. Are you likely to hurt yourself? Possibly—if you even get to the physical stage. At the very least, you might derail your progress by setting unrealistic goals.

The simple, brutal solution for the triathlon? Hit the gym and actually train.

For writing?

If you don't read, you are probably not going to be able to write readable stories. You can happily wank around with bad fanfiction and self-published shorts on Amazon, but the odds are not good on you winning a Nebula or Hugo Award. Or earning J.K. Rowling or E.L. James-levels of moolah. Who knows? You might. But the lottery's probably a better long shot.

One recent example was particularly salient: a person loftily asked whether the fantasy-reading world was ready for a mainstream fantasy book with an openly gay M/M relationship.

Within a couple of hours, other writers had offered links to several hundred mainstream recent and older SFF books with LGBT+ characters and relationships, and more discussion as to why it's no longer even a point of contention for many SFF publishers. Part of the discussion veered off into a snide rant about 'Pink SFF' being forced upon readers, and how manly men were hoping to reclaim spec fiction for the survival of the species (which was hilarious to read.)

The original poster was a bit stunned, but now has a reading list. And hopefully new inspiration.

All too often, when more seasoned writers gently point out that 1) the SFF community has been having a deep, wide-ranging dialog for over a century, and that 2) the Shiny Young Thing's shiny new world-changing idea is likely to be a familiar old trope...there is much gnashing of newbie teeth. Much flouncing and declamation of 'I am New! I am Shiny!' Or there is a disheartened and demoralized newbie creeping away, certain that nothing they create will amount to much, so why even try?

The best battle-plan falls somewhere in between. Ideas, after all, are ridiculously common. Most writers and artists have more ideas for projects than they can ever fulfill. What we do with ideas is more important: how we frame them, dress them up in philosophy or action, and make them uniquely ours.

If the problem is simple unfamiliarity, the new writer can read. Read Best-of lists and the best four or five-starred books on Amazon or Goodreads. Brush up on the critical skill of Research-Fu, and learn how to use Wikipedia, TV Tropes, and various compiled booklists to narrow down your focus. Take the books that spark your interest, and try to analyze them for what made them work. Not even the strongest speed-reader can hope to absorb a 100+ years of speculative fiction quickly, so it's wiser to take it slow, in easy portions. From there, you can go into writing exercises, revision tricks, how to research the publishing industry itself...

The best way to build a deep and believable 'world' for a fantasy or science fiction series? Research similar settings in real-world nonfictional books. Go deep. Fall down the rabbit-hole of responsible* research, and see where scholarship and science take you.

But it all starts with reading a book.

The same reaction also seems to come from writers between 55 and 75 of age, often male, often self-published, who haven't kept up with genres, technologies, and cultural changes. Several of the most entertaining recent AuthorFails have come from this group. It has happened enough that it's a solid data point in my Filigree's Rule checklist for authors-to-avoid.

* It pains me that I have to write this, but 'Do your own research' does not mean a quick glance at a conspiracy theory website, without having any background in how to research, and pulling only those data points that support your preconceived hypotheses. Learn a little of Research-Fu first, then grab a wide range of data from respected and documented sources.

Case Study 1: The Rise and (Fall?) of Erotic Romance

In the mid-to-late 1990s, most commercially published English-language romances had two big problems: they were white, and they were tame.

The need for diversity has caused clashes between younger and more-diverse writers and readers, and 'gatekeeper' writers' organizations like the Romance Writers of America (RWA). The RWA was infamous for being largely heterosexual, mostly older, and mostly white. There are welcome signs it's changing after near destruction in 2020, but the information and networking it offers have been mostly replaced by more-open online platforms.

Even the big romance convention gatherings are trimming membership or stopping altogether. Millennial and Gen-Z writers often simply can't afford conventions that can regularly cost over $1500 to attend. Framing them as taxable expenses isn't effective when writers are not making enough to take advantage of tax refunds months down the line.

The rise of self-publishing and prime fanfiction sources like Archive Of Our Own give readers cheaper or free outlets for erotic romance content.

More-enlightened science discoveries have validated the existence and normality of people on the Asexual gender spectrum, in all its variations. Aromantic, asexual, demisexual, and other aspects of this group offer one clue why sexual activity among younger populations seems to be falling: the excesses of the Free Love generation morphed into the cautious, HIV-aware 80s, and now give people an excuse to separate sex, romance, and various forms of celibacy. It's frankly a relief for many of us readers…but it doesn't mean we're not interested in sexy and romantic books!

It means we want *more* from those stories, than formulaic sexploits.

Is this the 'bust' end of a boom-or-bust cycle in romance and other genre publishing? It's probably just a pause before the industry morphs again. Unfortunately, that pause is devouring small publishers and their authors.

One of those romance sub-genres has been erotic romance: essentially, a romance where graphically-described sex is a foundational part of the plot, instead of the textual shorthand or fade-to-black techniques of older romance publishing.

Commercial sales are down throughout the e-pub romance industry. Amazon has an outsized thumb on the commercial scales. When they change advertising algorithms, small publishers can find advertising no longer works or is too expensive.

Informed self-publishing has taken a big bite out of both vanity and small-press publishing. Great authors are leaving their small publishers and striking out on their own…or are never even approaching those publishers.

Conventional heterosexual romance as a genre is soldiering on, but not as much in the commercial Big 4 realm. There, publishers seem to be scaling down their heterosexual romance lines. Judging by Manuscript Wish List and Publisher's Market announcements, literary agents are seeking fewer romance manuscripts. (Crossovers with other genres are a brighter exception.)

Erotic romance and LGBTQIA variants, as commercial sub-genres, are having an identity problem. Many of their writers (and readers) seem to be aging out. Following other demographic shifts, younger writers and readers may focusing on less overtly-sexualized content, with stronger emphasis on relationships and emotions.

Don't get me wrong: erotic romance is still a major player in both commercial and self-published work, and that is putting an ironic squeeze on the small-press publishers who were its champions for two decades.

One small-press publisher that broke ground and helped force the larger industry's change was Ellora's Cave, founded in 2000 and shut down by 2016.

A little history:

Erotic romance's 2000 to 2015 industry success may have come down to filling a niche at the right time. Conventional romance sex scenes were still largely fade-to-black or hilariously euphemized. SFF genre romance and romance-adjacent books were scarcely more open (after the Big 5 mostly erased a female-led Renaissance in the 1970s, '80s, and '90s).

Paranormal Romance exploded in the late 1990s. It offered crossover potential with science-fiction, fantasy, and mystery genres. PNR broke many of the old category romance taboos, boosting the bottom lines of many large commercial publishers with openly graphic heterosexual intimacy between characters.

Early 2000s erotic romance e-pubs like Ellora's Cave not only pushed for open sexual content in all these genres, they wanted *a lot of it*. Well before E. L. James rewrote Twilight fanfiction into a contemporary adult BDSM phenomenon, these publishers allowed writers and readers to experiment with all kinds of sexual variations between characters. Because of the new emphasis on sex and voracious readership demand, many of these books were written very quickly, with specific tropes, and sometimes at the expense of deeper plots or characters. (Not all! There are some stunning gems out there. Check the Look Inside option on any such Kindle book, and the first few pages will tell you which are which.)

On Amazon's Kindle Unlimited platform, more algorithm tweaks allowed the rise of shady practices like plagiarism, plot-mirroring (authors retell their own stories with different characters), book-stuffing (huge books filled with fake content to trick Amazon's Pages Read algorithm), bogus book collections, and traded/sold reviews...mostly in the erotic romance genre, where lower prices and big catalogs enticed readers.

As the erotic publishing revolution grew, commercial publishers took notice. They courted small-press erotic authors, and developed their own 'spicier' books and lines.

The Big 5 (possibly now Big 4, with consolidation) romance & SFF publishers have now discovered that diversity sells, so they're tentatively adding POC and/or LGBTQIA books to their normal roster, often with a larger dose of graphically-described sex.

All of these issues can spell doom for a small-press erotic romance publisher.

Follow the math. To paraphrase a recent Twitter thread, an e-publisher usually pays a 40% royalty on every book sale. That means they hold 60% of that sale to pay overhead and bank for profit. The 40% should always be sequestered from general funds. In small-press reality, it often mingles with the general fund, and might be siphoned off on other expenses.

If the publisher overdraws their 60% and pulls from what should be the authors' cut, that can lead to a dangerous and potentially illegal downward spiral. Without serious financial intervention, the company can never catch up to its ongoing debts.

Paying editors on royalties-only is another danger sign, which can lead to equal damage to a publisher.

What does this mean to eager new erotic romance authors trying to 'break in' to the erotic romance field?

Do serious research on publishers before you submit anything to a small press publisher.

Understand that the world of small-press erotic romance is a big gamble. Even the best small publisher can have an unexpected meltdown.

In exchange for (at best) a stunning cover and decent editing, most small-press writers are going to get an early push of blog marketing and some Advance Reader Copies (usually too late to gather any wide industry notice), and desultory marketing afterward. Most small-press romance books will sell no more than $1000 to $1500 in their first few years of publication. Some have dangerously-strict contracts that leave the author exposed to difficulty in submitting work elsewhere, or getting rights back if the publisher fails to sell their work (or goes out of business.)

Writing more books to build a back-catalog seems to help, as does responsible social media marketing and self-promotion.

Writing better books and seeking a capable literary agent (yes, they still exist, and they're still looking for great cross-genre books) can help springboard you into the bigger commercial publishing world (which has its own pitfalls).

Seriously look into self-publishing at least some of your work.

Train for and keep a decent day-job, if you can. Writers don't usually get benefits, and most of them earn far below minimum wage at writing. There is absolutely no real stigma in not writing full-time, or taking a break from writing. Anyone who tells you otherwise is either stupid or a classist hypocrite. It's a dirty not-so-secret that many 'successful' creative people have outside funding.

I would tell you 'Don't give up', but every person has their limits. I do hope you don't give up on sharing your dreams and your voice.

Whatever you do, don't pay a vanity publisher. If you can use the internet, you can self-publish, instead!

THERE HAVE BEEN REAMS written about the specific rise and fall of Ellora's Cave. You can plug that name into Wikipedia, and get the low-down.

Its trajectory is a classic example of Publisher Fail. From explosive growth in authors signed, readerships, and earnings in 2000-2010, the publisher gradually fell prey to the following problems:

Poor or no accounting. Authors were seeing longer and longer periods without royalty statements or payments. Those statements seemed more and more opaque, with missing or incomplete sales data.

Publisher personal problems. The main owner of Ellora's Cave appeared to be using publishing income to fund personal debts and expenses, without setting aside money for company debts. Tax liens show multiple failures to pay state income tax.

Nonpayment of contracted editors and artists.

Legal fights with bloggers and reviewers, including some ill-advised suits that appeared to show the publisher was even more at fault than critics had claimed.

Losing authors by the dozens in the 2013-2015 years, the publisher created large 'rights release' fees that could climb to six figures when authors wanted to buy out their contracts.

I use Ellora's Cave as a cautionary example to keep tabs on publishers over multiple years. Situations can change, and old information may not be accurate anymore.

Case Study 2: Tate Publishing

Let's look back at Tate Publishing, as a company deeply interlocked with nominally 'Christian' Dominionist worldviews that enshrine greed, corruption, hatred-of-others, and the Prosperity Gospel belief that poverty is a moral failing.

Prosperity Gospel philosophy bluntly preaches that wealth and success are outward signs of God's favor, and that poverty and illness are signs of his disfavor and/or a flawed person. 'Anyone can become successful' is an innate American ideal, but these days the game is often rigged against lower-class and lower-middle-class workers. The proponents of the Prosperity Gospel tend to cleverly repackage their corruption to shunt public attention away from their own greed and hypocrisy.

Many multi-level marketing companies, mega-churches, and vanity publishers have similar goals: to enrich a small percentage of their members/founders at the expense of all others, and to instill a cult-like level of support from those same defrauded members.

Perhaps no other American vanity publishing company took the religious overtones to such extremes as Oklahoma's Tate Publishing. Its business model has been copied outright and adapted by many other religiously-affiliated publishers.

It was started by Dr. Richard Tate and his wife Rita about two decades ago, and has been run recently by son Ryan Tate and his wife Christy.

The Tate family leveraged new technology and new social norms to begin marketing their pay-for-publishing business to primarily Christian authors, artists, and musicians. They promised a wholesome Christian outlook, a supportive 'family' experience, well-produced physical books and music recordings, state-of-the-industry marketing...all for a hefty front end 'subsidy' from the author, as well as a commission charge on all sales.

How hefty? Authors could pay anywhere from almost $4000 to well over $50,000 depending on what 'marketing packages' and other promotional frills Tate's aggressive sales people could convince them to buy.

Tate's book editing was often done by low-skilled, underpaid, and in some cases even outsourced foreign editors. Covers were often low-quality, as were interior illustrations. Tate's marketing of finished products was nearly non-existent, and for the large part ineffective for most authors.

Many of these authors were told various forms of 'buy the books from us, and hand-sell at local events'. This naturally limits an author's effective sell-rate, as most people can only reach a few hundred of their family and friends. Effective trade publishers market to much broader groups, and generally command much higher sales.

Victoria Strauss of Writer Beware wrote a few years ago:

*'Tate takes pains to **depict itself as a selective traditional publisher** that accepts "only a single-digit percentage of authors who submitted manuscripts for publication" (a claim that's a little hard to credit from a publisher that, **if Amazon is to be believed**, pumped out 3,000 titles in 2015). In fact, authors must pay nearly $4,000 to publish with Tate, with even more due if they choose to buy any of Tate's array of extras, such as "personalized author websites" and video book trailers. Tate also incentivizes author book-buying, by promising to refund the original fee once 2,500 books are sold and allowing author purchases to count toward the total—though only if made in bulk quantities of 300 or more.'*

Of course, Tate never mentioned these fees in its front-end website material or videos. Only when authors asked for more information or submitted a manuscript, did Tate begin to disclose its fees. If authors balked at the cost, the the sales rep often backtracked to 'offer' a lesser amount. Authors were stalked with hard-sell tactics including multiple letters, emails, and phone calls, all to close the sale.

Tate representatives also didn't disclose the very small probability of any author making enough sales to earn a refund of their original fee.

Tate's main source of income appeared not to be consumer sales of their books and music, but book and music sales to their author/creators and expensive marketing and other packages.

Authors couldn't even be certain of what they were actually earning, because Tate's royalty accounting was so opaque as to be nearly meaningless. Authors complained that they diligently marketed their books, knew of documented sales, and collected testimonials from readers...and yet did not see those sales reflected in royalty reports.

This could be seen as early as 2004. While the warnings abounded, Tate never lacked for customers to buy its 'services', thanks to the enduring power of religious affinity fraud.

Because Tate marketed heavily to fundamentalist Christians who were already put off by 'coastal elites' and 'Jewish mainstream publishers', they could conceal their less-savory operations from unsuspecting authors who never bothered to learn how commercial publishing worked.

Tate Publishing also marketed heavily to senior citizens wanting a retirement income or a family history project in print, to misery memoir authors wanting to memorialize a lost loved one or bring attention to a medical issue, and to 'fringe group' believers who might not have the writing skills to reach an audience through a big trade publishing imprint.

Here's the opening story of a typical Tate author, revealing how she was conned by Tate:

'When Tate first called me, it was like I had won the lottery! I felt so proud of becoming one of the 4%. My children's book was special, as it was written after my daughter had her 2nd heart surgery. I was filling a niche. I knew it would be hard to publish a children's book about Down Syndrome, but I had tried and succeeded.'

This author had a noble cause and good faith in Tate's public persona. She didn't research enough to understand Tate's failings before signing a contract with them. She did all the right things by industriously marketing herself at Down's Syndrome support events across the US. But she received no marketing help from Tate after the first couple of months, and her royalty checks ranged from sixty-some dollars to forty-two cents.

Tate authors were often warned away from naysayers as 'negative influences' and 'liars'.

The Tate family were quick to take offense and threatened critics, bad reviewers, and recalcitrant authors with libel lawsuits. They threatened their employees often, and had a high turnover as disillusioned editors and artists fled the company.

Of about 1000 current authors in the 2016 Tate catalog, Ryan Tate claimed most were 'very happy'. I'd believe it, if only for the power of Sunk Cost Fallacy and even perhaps Stockholm Syndrome. Many people never want to admit they've been conned, and go through mental gymnastics to avoid it. Likewise, authors who never know anything different might be happy with poor marketing, vague royalty statements, and tiny sales. For some people, it's not about the money, but having something in print.

Here too, Tate failed a lot of writers. Many of the Consumer Affairs complaints involve claims of shoddy books, bad covers and illustrations, or simply no physical books produced.

Even when authors finally wised up and tried to leave the company, Tate Publishing had one last con to play: they charged authors a $50.00 'processing fee' to turn over final print/sound files so the authors and musicians could republish their work. (Rights buy-backs are a huge problem in the vanity and small-press publishing industry). Because Tate's final fee wasn't large, many unhappy authors simply paid it and moved on...often to similar vanity publishers!

A few years ago, driven mostly by the attrition of their prime senior citizen clients and the advent of easier digital self-publishing, Tate Publishing fell on hard times. They started outsourcing much of their editing and other production work overseas. There's a famous rant online from when Ryan Tate fired 25 employees after none of them told who leaked their dissent about the outsourcing.

Soon, Tate couldn't even pay its foreign workers in the Philippines, and 'scaled back production' returned to their Oklahoma facilities. Bear in mind, they still released thousands of books and hundreds of records a year, showing how little money and time actually went into production. Authors who visited the Tate offices at this time described the formerly busy company as 'a ghost town'. High employee turnover caused communication breakdowns between authors, staff, and company officials.

By mid 2016, Tate Publishing's lease deals with major print machinery and computer suppliers were on the rocks, leading to at least one hefty

lawsuit.   *https://victoriastrauss.com/2016/06/16/*
tate-publishing-enterprises-slapped-with-1-7-million-lawsuit-department-of-

By late 2016 there were at least 800 complaints being considered by the Oklahoma Attorney General's office, and thousands of warnings by disgruntled authors and ex-Tate employees across the internet.

First, the Tates announced that they might open up again. The OK AG office was understandably reluctant to add more names to its case files against Tate, so they charged the Tate patriarch Richard and his son Ryan with felony embezzlement charges, misdemeanor embezzlement charges, and three felony attempted extortion by threat charges.

Those last charges, the extortions? All come back to those $50 processing fees, which were apparently paid to Tate Publishing but funneled to the Tate family's private bank accounts. A day after the charges were made public Richard and Ryan Tate were arrested, held on $100,000 bond each, and forced to surrender their passports.

See   also: *https://www.theyukonreview.com/2019/07/27/*
list-of-victims-for-tate-publishing-finalized/

The Tate family announced in late 2016 that it would close its doors, but not without hinting they would simply rename the company and rise as a new publisher.

By 2020, the Tate's tax refunds had been intercepted by the Oklahoma Attorney General. The family had been accused of using some authors' money to buy drugs and gamble at casinos. The Tates are on the hook for at least $900,000 in restitution to their authors and other creditors.

Here is the Wikipedia article on the company and its owners: *https://en.wikipedia.org/wiki/Tate_Publishing_%26_Enterprises*

Here's a Writers Weekly article with more current information: *https://writersweekly.com/angela-desk/ tax-refunds-of-tate-publishings-owners-will-be-intercepted-by-the-oklahoma-atto*

There will be authors who still champion Tate Publishing. There are still plenty of fully-operational vanity publishers, some even modeled after Tate, ready to take their money and dreams.

(This section compiled from information courtesy of newsok.com, koko.com, Writer Beware, Publishers Weekly, Writers Weekly, Wikipedia, and consumeraffairs.com.)

Afterthoughts

I hope this book helped show you some publishing danger signs.

As I've said before, I'm moving from small-press to self-publishing with a bunch of manuscripts I have piled up. Mostly because these are in a loose fantasy series that can't be queried now, since too many of the books were previously published.

Getting them out into the world seemed more useful than simply trunking them.

I'm not counting on becoming a self-publishing titan, since I earn my living in other fields.

I am fond of commercial publishing, more so now that it's moving in more progressive directions. When I have a standalone, unrelated manuscript (fiction or nonfiction), I will certainly be querying it to literary agents first.

Remember: *how* you publish (with the exception of vanity publishing) is less important now. If you have a great book you believe in, and you've done the work to make it as professional and readable as possible...

Publish wisely!

Don't miss out!

Visit the website below and you can sign up to receive emails whenever M. Crane Hana publishes a new book. There's no charge and no obligation.

https://books2read.com/r/B-A-HIMI-MRCOB

BOOKS 2 READ

Connecting independent readers to independent writers.

Also by M. Crane Hana

The Lonhra Sequence
Bloodshadow
The Purist
Saints and Heroes
Moro's Price

Standalone
The Blood Orange Tree
Maestro
Filigree's Rule

Watch for more at https://www.cranehanabooks.com.

About the Author

As M. Crane Hana, I write erotic romance, high fantasy, and space fantasy.

As Marian Crane, I'm known for jewelry design, book sculpture, and fiber arts.

As Filigree, I make trouble online.

Read more at https://www.cranehanabooks.com.